D1366663

RETIREMENT READINESS

YOUR ROADMAP TO A SUCCESSFUL JOURNEY

TERRY E. DUPONT, CPhD, CRPS

As Seen On

This document discusses general concepts for retirement planning, and is not intended to provide tax or legal advice. Individuals are urged to consult with their tax and legal professionals regarding these issues. This handbook should ensure that clients understand a) that annuities and some of their features have costs associated with them; b) that income received from annuities is taxable; and c) that annuities used to fund IRAs do not afford any additional measure of tax deferral for the IRA owner.

Printed in the United States of America

First Printing, 2014

Gradient Positioning Systems, LLC
4105 Lexington Avenue North, Suite 110
Arden Hills, MN 55126 (877) 901-0894

Contributors: Nick Stovall, Nate Lucius, Mike Binger and Gradient Positioning Systems, LLC.

Gradient Positioning Systems, LLC and Terry Dupont are not affiliated with or endorsed by the Social Security Administration or any government agency.

ACKNOWLEDGEMENTS

First and foremost, I would like to thank my Lord and Savior for blessing me with the gifts of a servant heart, the passion and joy of trying to help secure the financial future of mature Americans every day, and the wisdom to do the next right thing.

I would like to thank my mother and father, Carl and Millie DuPont, for instilling an entrepreneurial spirit in me at a young age, whether they realized they were doing it or not.

I would like to thank my pastor and good friend, J.P. Freeman, for his wisdom, life guidance, and love and joy for leading others on the road less traveled.

I would like to thank Amanda Neal, my assistant, para-planner, and business partner for adopting my zeal for the pursuit of excellence and client satisfaction, and following our code to under-promise and over-deliver.

I would like to thank our entire professional team and support staff for putting up with my demands for excellence on a daily basis.

I would like to thank all of our valued clients for their trust in us and for their loyalty.

Last, but not least, I would like to thank Carol Jean Butler for her professionalism and assistance in putting my thoughts and ramblings into written word.

This book is dedicated to everyone who wonders if their current advisors are giving them the best advice possible and that which is in their best interest, to those that want to ensure that their golden years are just that... truly golden, and to the charities that benefit from the proceeds of this book.

May God shower all of you with an overflow of blessings.

TABLE OF CONTENTS

INTRODUCTION

It's hard to see the picture when you're inside the frame.

Jeff's parents lived and worked in the same town for 35 years. They paid off the house and had no credit card debt. They also had no 401(k), no IRA and no financial professional to help them with their retirement plan because the plan was simple: claim your Social Security benefit, receive your company pension and stop working!

Jeff's father got a gold watch, a party, and a pension that generated regular, monthly paychecks; his mother also received a Social Security check from the part-time work she did. His parents didn't have to worry about whether or not the money would be there because their benefits weren't exposed to stock market risk. They didn't have to worry about making investment decisions, diversifying their assets, or planning for tax strategies. Their income was guaranteed and when it came time to file for Social Security, they had only two choices: file or don't file.

1

As Jeff plans for his retirement, he finds that things are much more complicated today. For one example, he doesn't have a guaranteed pension; he has multiple 401(k) plans because he has worked for a few different companies. He knows his hard earned savings are invested in stock market funds, but he has no idea how much risk those investments are exposed to or how they can provide an income for him. His wife, Karen, also has a 401(k), and she is invested in preferred stock for the company she works for. A few years ago, Karen also inherited her father's IRA. Jeff wants to use the money to pay off the house so they will not have a mortgage payment during retirement, but they wonder, would doing that result in a tax event? Would they be better off moving the IRA into a different investment? And if so, what is the right investment? Karen is just turning 60, and Jeff is 62 and currently eligible to receive Social Security. Karen thinks he should file now and start claiming the money, but is now the best time to file?

A lot of retirees, like Jeff and Karen, have a lot of decisions to make about the future of their retirement. Just in filing their Social Security benefits, a married couple today has over 4,900 different filing options and thousands of dollars in lifetime benefits they stand to gain or lose. With multiple retirement accounts, conflicting advice about investments, and safe withdrawal rates it is hard to know what are smart choices to make with your retirement savings. You can't watch T.V. or read a newspaper today without being reminded of the uncertain times we're in, the stock market volatility, massive deficits, escalating health care costs and the overall rising cost of living. If you compound all of that with the fact that today's retirees are living longer (19 years longer for men and 15 years longer for women according to the Social Security Administration) you understand why today's retirees are facing a crisis of epic proportion.

With all these big decisions towering in front of them, aspiring retirees can't see the forest through the trees. With so many variables in play, when does a person ever feel ready to retire?

Retiring today involves thousands of options and multiple working parts. One wrong decision can put the stability of your retirement lifestyle at peril. What's worse is most retirees aren't even aware of the risk they are taking when it comes to the security of their Retirement income. Retired life is or soon will be your everyday life. Are you ready? Do you have a plan that supports the life you want to live? Do you have a plan that you can get behind?

An entire industry exists today, one that didn't exist during the time when Jeff's parent's retired. This industry is dedicated to doing the one thing that Jeff's parents never had to worry about: Retirement Planning.

THE RETIREMENT PLANNING 8-BALL: ARE YOU BEHIND IT?

Today's Baby Boomers are not retiring to their rocking chairs; instead they have places they want to go. With increasing longevity, has come increasing health and vigor, new ideas about what retiring really means. What do you want to be doing during your retirement? Where do you want to go? And with whom do you want to be doing these things?

Retirement planning gives you a unique opportunity to design a roadmap for the next ten, twenty, even thirty years of your life. This journey can be a great adventure or a great disappointment, depending on how well you plan for it! You might envision one thing today but want something different five years down the road. You might do everything right, but unexpectedly hit a "bump," "detour on the road," or even a road block that throws off your entire plan. Change **is** part of retirement life, which is why any plan designed to support you must be flexible.

A good retirement plan (your roadmap) will help organize all the pieces of the puzzle so you can see through the trees to the forest, field, mountains, and beyond. The financial professional who helps you run the numbers and choose the right investments is like your personal tour guide who can get you through your retirement years safely, with all your goals and dreams intact.

During your working years, retirement planning is a pretty easy process: you simply put away as much money as you can in an IRA, 401(k), 403b or whatever you choose, and hope for the best. Once you enter the retirement years, planning becomes much more complex. There are no more regular paychecks coming from your employer, and for most retirees, pensions have gone the way of the dinosaurs, which means the investments necessary for generating a regular paycheck now rely on you. As you move out of the accumulation and earning stage, you enter into the Distribution Stage. The Distribution Stage is when you are now relying on the viability of those investments and savings to provide income for you. Do you know which investments to take that money from? Are those investments secure enough to support you for 10 to 30 years down the road? If you are lucky enough to have a pension, do you know how to maximize that pension and what your survivor options are?

Simply retiring like our parents did and pulling the trigger on one of your income sources without looking at all the working parts, such as how that income will be taxed, can have severe and debilitating repercussions. The biggest fear for almost all retirees today is running out of money. One wrong decision about your money during this stage of life can jeopardize the ability of your income to support you during the 5 to 30 year time frame known as the golden years. The biggest influencer as to whether or not those years truly will be golden has everything to do with the quality of your plan. **All of the pieces of the puzzle need to be integrated into a cohesive whole in order to maximize efficien-**

cies, increase net worth, and provide a sustainable, predictable income for life. You can have the retirement of your dreams if you take the time to create the roadmap that can help you get there.

FIVE COMPONENTS OF A SUCCESSFUL RETIREMENT ROADMAP

Most people worry about the ability of their savings to provide an adequate income during their retirement, but income alone isn't the only component of a good plan. There are other working parts that affect the longevity of your income and the ability of your hard-earned dollars to support you. These working parts can be boiled down to the following five main categories: income, investments, health care, taxes, and legacy/estate planning. Within the pages of this book, you'll find the information you need when making decisions within each of these five areas. While everyone's plan is different and must be tailor-made to fit your individual needs, what follows is a readiness checklist of the things every retiree should consider when designing their plan.

Retirement Income

- Have you maximized your known sources of income such as your Social Security and pension benefits?
- Do you have a guaranteed, safe and sustainable income for the rest of your life?
- Does your income plan protect you from the ravages of inflation?
- Are the investments you rely on for income protected from volatile stock market loss?
- Have you taken steps to protect this income for your surviving spouse?

Investment Choices

- Do you know why you own the investments that you own?
- Do you know exactly how much risk you are undertaking?
- Are your investments accomplishing exactly what you want and need?
- Are you aware of the in-service withdrawal option on your 401(k) account?
- Can your retirement savings survive another stock market decline?

Health Care Considerations

- Have you protected your assets from the devastating costs of health care?
- Is your spouse protected in the event of a chronic or disabling illness?
- Do you have strategies in place that provide for long term professional in-home or facility care?

Tax Repercussions

- Are you paying unnecessary income taxes?
- Do you have an IRA exit strategy?
- Are your investments allocated for optimum tax efficiency?

Estate and Legacy

- Do you have an updated Will, Durable Power of Attorney, Health Care Power of Attorney, and Indiana Transfer on Death documents?
- Do you know what your estate tax liability is?
- Do you want your spouse and heirs to receive your assets taxable or tax-free?

YOUR FINANCIAL ADVOCATE

According to a 2013 Wells Fargo study, middle-class Americans who had a written retirement plan in place accumulated three times as much retirement assets as compared to those who didn't have a plan in place.* There are a lot of people out there who can offer you investment advice, but not everybody is in the business of comprehensive retirement planning.

DuPont Wealth Management offers customized asset protection and sustained income solutions for retirees, aspiring retirees, and their families. Our trained staff includes experts who are knowledgeable in every area of the retirement planning process from our healthcare specialist to our chief tax strategist. Our firm offers the Social Security Optimization Report and the Retirement Income Analysis on a complimentary basis because as a faith-based organization, we believe this information is too valuable not to share and we see this as one way we can give back to our community. The information these reports provide can prevent you from making huge financial mistakes, and they are one way you can give our firm a "test drive" to see what it might be like to join our client family.

Retirement is a journey fraught with challenging decisions, tax codes, and regulations and rules (some of which change annually). It's hard to know what to do or what impact your decisions will have on the big picture when you're stuck inside the frame. When working with a trained professional who is held to a fiduciary standard it means having someone by your side that will look objectively at your situation and offer recommendations as your financial advocate. When you work with us here at DuPont Wealth Management, you become more than just another client,

---

https://www.wellsfargo.com/about/press/2013/20131023_middleclasssurvey

you become a member of the family, and that means you don't have to go on the retirement journey alone.

— Terry E. DuPont, Retirement Income Specialist, Private Wealth Advisor and President and CEO of DuPont & Associates, Inc, and DuPont Wealth Management, a Registered Investment Advisor firm.

1

WHAT YOU WANT AND WHERE YOU WANT TO GO

*"More than 90 percent of today's Boomers feel the U.S. is facing a retirement crisis, and more retirees fear outliving their money more than they fear death."**

Money represents more than the paper it's printed on. It is the embodiment of your time, your talents, and your commitments. It buys the food you eat, the house you sleep in, the car you drive, and the clothes you wear. It also helps provide you with the lifestyle you want to live once you retire.

---

*http://www.pensionrights.org/publications/fact-sheet/polling-data-americas-retirement-crisis

You spend your entire working life hoping what you put into your retirement accounts will help you live comfortably once you clock out of the workforce for the last time. The key word in that sentiment and the word that can make retirement feel like a looming problem instead of a rewarding life stage, is *hope*. You *hope* you will have enough money.

Leaving your retirement up to chance is unadvisable by nearly any standard, yet millions of people find themselves *hoping* instead of planning for a happy ending. The biggest fear of retirees today is running out of money, but retirement should be the time in your life when you get to enjoy your money. What do you want to do during retirement? What is your current lifestyle? Would you like to maintain that lifestyle, or are there changes you would like to make?

Most clients find that if they take the time to move through the planning phase and answer these important questions about goals, needs and wants, not only can they achieve stability of income, they can also achieve the retirement of their dreams. How is this possible? Simply by taking the "*Hope So*" out your retirement and placing it with "*Know So*", guaranteed sources of income.

WHERE ARE YOU AT NOW?

You've spent your entire life saving for this rewarding stage of your life. The plan you develop should be based on more than just investments and financial products; a retirement plan should begin with where you are now and what's important to you.

A financial professional who has your best interest in mind won't sell you an investment product or service until they get to know you first. He or she will ask questions designed to consider your current lifestyle and hopes for future years. Your personal goals must come before the assets because until we know what you want your retirement to look like, we can't make appropriate investment recommendations.

What do you envision your retirement will look like? What are you doing? Where are you doing it? And with whom are you doing it? Does the retirement you envision include starting a business, working part time, moving and relocating, volunteer work, a new hobby, a vacation home, travel abroad or going back to school? One of the first questions to address as you approach retirement planning is whether or not you are ready to stop working.

Where Are You at Regarding Work?
- Have you maximized your 401(k) contributions?
- Have you considered the relationships you have with co-workers and how you might miss that interaction?
- Do you know the age at which you would like to retire?
- Do you have a good sense of whether or not you can retire when you'd like to?
- Will you work during retirement?
- Do you know which of your skills could easily be transferred to a new part-time job?

Once you gain clarity about your work situation, questions turn to lifestyle. It might make sense to downsize and sell the house for an apartment in the city. Or, conversely, it might make sense to save money by moving out of the city and renting or buying a cottage in the country. How much income you need during retirement depends on these lifestyle plans.

What Does Your Retirement Lifestyle Look Like?
- Is living near your children or grandchildren important?
- Where does your spouse want to live during retirement? Do you share similar ideas?
- Have you thought about what you're going to do on the day that you retire?

- Do you have a hobby or sport you would like to pursue that will keep you busy?
- Do you have a plan for how to spend your weekdays when you are no longer working full-time?
- Have you thought about volunteering or other ways to keep your mind sharp?
- Have you and your spouse defined the lifestyle you want to maintain during retirement?
- Are you willing to reduce your standard of living during retirement in order to retire sooner?

Once you identify the when and where, it's time to talk about the who. Who do you see yourself spending time with during your retirement years? Will you be sharing living expenses? Will you be traveling to visit family and friends? One of the more surprising aspects of retirement for married couples is the daily interaction that occurs once both parties are no longer working. This might be a welcome arrangement for some; others might find themselves constructing a studio or workshop in the garage. While this is said somewhat facetiously, it does help to talk about the relationships important to you during this new phase in your life.

What Relationships Are Important During Retirement?
- Have you discussed with your spouse how your day-to-day activities might interact together?
- Is your family aware of your goals, dreams and interests for retirement?
- Does your family have any expectations of financial support during your retirement years?
- Do you want to leave an inheritance to your children or grandchildren?

When deciding whether or not an investment is a good fit for a client, these are the core considerations that can help a professional determine which investment tools are the best for the longevity of your income plan. If these sound like personal questions, it's because they are. Planning for retirement isn't just about the numbers; it's about the people behind the numbers, namely you. If your retirement plan doesn't take into account your goals and retirement dreams, then it won't be a plan that can carry you through to your journey's end.

WHERE DO YOU WANT TO BE?

It is the savings you have acquired that will fund your retirement journey, taking you from where you are now to where you will be in five years, 10 years, or even 30 years down the road. How you manage that money largely dictates the success of your journey. Advice about what to do with money has been around as long as money has existed. While there are some basic investment concepts that have stood the test of time, most strategies that work adapt to changing conditions in the market, in the economy, and the world, as well as changes in your personal circumstances. Low CD rates combined with market volatility have made it difficult to predict the future. How do you choose investments when planning for 30 years down the road with this much uncertainty?

The reality is that investment strategies and savings plans that worked in the past have encountered challenging new circumstances. One such financial theory is the *buy and hold* strategy practiced by index fund money managers. In a 2012 CNN Money Magazine interview, economist and finance Professor Andrew Lo explains why buy and hold doesn't work anymore: *"The volatility is too significant. Almost any asset can suddenly become much more risky. Buying a mutual fund and holding onto it for 10 years is no longer going to deliver the same kind of expected return we saw over the course of the last seven decades, simply because of the nature of financial markets and how complex it's gotten."*

The Great Recession of the early 2000's highlighted how old investment ideas were not only ineffective but incredibly destructive to the retirement plans of millions of Americans. The dawn of an entirely restructured health care system brings with it new options and challenges that will undoubtedly change the way insurance companies provide investment products and services. Perhaps the most important lessons investors have learned is that not understanding where your money is invested (and the potential risks of those investments) can work against you, your plans for retirement and your legacy. Saving and investing money isn't enough to truly get the most out of it. You must have a planful approach to managing your assets.

Essentially, managing your money and your investments is an ongoing process that requires customization and adaptation to a changing world. And make no mistake; the world is always changing. What worked for your parents or even your parents' parents was probably good advice back then. People in retirement or approaching retirement today need new ideas and professional guidance.

WHO WILL HELP YOU GET THERE?

In light of news headlines about fraud, Ponzi schemes and a lack of regulatory oversight, it's important to educate yourself about the differences between working with financial professionals who are sales people and those who are retirement planners. There are six main differences you need to be aware of when selecting who you will trust with the intimate financial details of your retirement future. These six differences begin with the most important difference:

Fiduciary vs. Suitability

The legal standards by which each type of provider is measured are quite significant and have a direct bearing on what investments they recommend and how your portfolio is structured. A professional held to suitability standards can sell you anything as long as it's considered suitable. The word "suitable" can invite a lot of gray area. For example, some people might consider a bag of potato chips to be a suitable lunch while others, moms especially, would most certainly disagree. A professional held to fiduciary standards is legally obligated to recommend products and services that are in your best interests. While you can still eat the potato chips if you want to, a fiduciary professional is obligated to recommend the healthier choices that would be in your best interest.

Black's Law Dictionary describes a fiduciary relationship as *"one founded on trust or confidence reposed by one person in the integrity and fidelity of another."* Law.com defines a fiduciary as "a person who has the power and obligation to act for another under circumstances which require total trust, good faith and honesty." According to the National Association of Personal Financial Advisors (*NAPFA*), a fiduciary is required to act with undivided loyalty to the client, which includes disclosure of how the financial advisor is to be compensated and any corresponding conflicts of interest.'

As a Registered Investment Advisor under the Investment Advisers Act of 1940, RIAs are required to act as a fiduciary. These professionals must put your interests above their own and declare any conflicts of interest that may arise. For example, if they were selling potato chips manufactured by their Uncle Herb, they would be legally obligated to reveal this fact. You can be assured the portfolio an RIA constructs is designed to meet your goals and put your interests above all else. On the other hand, a broker, or Registered Representative, is required only to recommend investments that are "suitable" for you. They can legally put their own interest above yours when recommending investments as long as that investment can be considered suitable for the situation.

Advice vs. Transactions

Since brokers are paid by commissions on products sold, there is also a subtle pressure to do transactions. For example, if your broker receives a 10 percent commission on every bag of potato chips he sells, then you can bet those chips will come highly recommended. Keep in mind that brokerage firms are usually investment product manufacturers who view their broker employees as the prime distribution channel for selling their products. In other words, your broker is working for the company that produces the chips.

On the other hand, RIAs are typically paid an advisory fee directly from the client for advice and services provided, usually based on a percentage of the assets under their care. RIAs have no incentive to sell or recommend you any one product or investment over another, which is why they are free to make recommendations that are in your best interest. This reduces or eliminates the inherent conflict of interest most brokers experience when working within the structure of their brokerage firms.

Transparency vs. Disclosure

Brokers usually follow the rules for legal disclosures by providing their clients with prospectus booklets and voluminous, lengthy legal documents printed in small-type and written in highly formal legalese language. This has become standard disclosure practice for the brokerage industry, but how many people actually sit down to read the prospectus books on their investments? And if they do read them, how much is understandable?

RIAs adhere to a higher standard of transparency designed to give you meaningful, relevant, and straightforward information. The book you are holding in your hand is one example of our intent to educate and serve. Fiduciary professionals fully share details about any aspect of their services and how they earn their fees. Clients receive quarterly reports with all RIA fees clearly listed, and as custodians of your assets, they will also report these fees on your account statements for comparison. Most RIAs do not take any commissions or "marketing incentives" from investment product providers. In other words, even if they do sell a bag of Uncle Herb's chips, they are not allowed to accept remuneration. However, some RIAs are also licensed brokers and insurance agents, which would enable them to receive a commission on products sold. Your RIA's disclosure statement will offer explanations on what, if any, types of product commissions they may receive.

Registered Investment Advisor vs. Investment/Financial Advisor
Over the past 10 to 15 years, many brokers have begun to use the title of "Wealth Manager," "Investment Advisor" or "Financial Advisor" without accepting the fiduciary duty of a Registered Investment Advisor as described in the Investment Advisers Act of 1940. These self-appointment titles can be very confusing to an investor looking for a professional they can trust. Some "Wealth Managers" or "Advisors" have no real background or training with regard to giving financial advice other than the sales training they have received. Most merely adhere to the "suitability" doctrine.

In the past, some very large, household-name brokerages have lobbied Congress to avoid the fiduciary level of accountability being imposed on their brokers. Not surprisingly, it's common to find that the "suitable" investments recommended by the professional to be those that pay the broker and his employer the highest fees for the sale of these products; but more than that, as a client you are likely not getting the holistic advice you need. The line between broker-dealer and investment advisor is further blurred by the invention and bundling of new products such as "Wrap" programs and "Fee-Based" platforms that make it difficult to distinguish fee structures. Because of the diversity of these products and services, investors often fail to recognize the difference between brokers and investment advisors and as a result, they don't get the comprehensive investment advice they truly need to design a retirement plan.

Safe Money Specialists Dedicated to Your Financial Prosperity & Success

Another safeguard RIAs employ is the use of third party custodians for your assets. When you purchase an investment from an RIA, your accounts are typically placed with a major custodian and not held in-house at the RIA. This offers you greater protection because the RIA in some cases retains some control over the funds held by these third party custodians. He or she may be able to buy and sell securities on your behalf, move funds between your accounts, and have funds sent directly to you via your address of record or like-registered account. This practice was not employed by the firms involved in most of the recent fraud or Ponzi schemes. Typically, the firms involved in those fraudulent schemes had direct control of the vast majority of assets under management and direct control of most of the information about those assets (meaning generation of all statements, audit information, and periodic update materials). Those practices greatly facilitated the embezzlement and fraud. By using a third party custodian, clients are able to verify account information provided by an RIA against statements provided by custodians, thus enhancing security and providing a check-and-balance.

Ethics vs. Law

Even though more stringent regulations are under consideration by our government, unethical behavior cannot be legislated out of existence. Registered Investment Advisors believe the best way to earn your trust is through sound advice and an open relationship. No matter what regulatory standards are decided by our government institutions regarding brokerage firms and their accountability, the majority of quality RIAs always accept their fiduciary responsibility to clients. The ethics and values RIAs have for how they serve clients are higher than any legal standard. At the core of these values is the concept of fiduciary duty and a pledge to never compromise the difference between investment advice that is in your best interest and advice that **is not.**

As a retiree, once you understand the six main differences between working with a professional that is held to fiduciary standards versus suitability standards, you will understand why Warren Buffet is well known for saying, *"Run, don't walk, if you are working with a broker."*

FROM GO-GO TO NO-GO

When making decisions about investments, it helps to get a big-picture understanding of what those investments will be used for. Retirement is a long journey and most retirees find that they pass through three distinct phases. Each phase presents different financial challenges that you will want to be prepared for in order to get the most enjoyment out of that particular time. If you are beginning the planning process during your retirement, it can be helpful to identify your current stage as you begin to organize and understand your assets.

The Go-Go Phase: As a retiree you are no longer working, but you find that you are just as busy. You're still feeling young, strong, and your directive is to get going on all the things you've always wanted to do but never before had the time. Now you've got the time and the energy; and with proper planning, you can ensure ample funds to support your ambitions. Whether it's spending time with the grandkids or seeing the world, you will want to budget appropriately for this fun and rewarding stage of your retirement.

The Go-Slow Phase: You have gotten a lot done and no longer have the traveling bug (or maybe you never had it in the first place.) You are still healthy and active but it feels right to start slowing things down. Maybe it's that you are appreciating things more deeply, or maybe you just don't feel the need to be in such a hurry. Regardless of the why, this usually happens sometime in your mid-70s and it can be a peaceful time of enriched experiences and relationships. If you are in this phase of your retirement, it's a good time to take stock of what's ahead and make sure you are prepared financially.

The No-Go Phase: As you enjoy the increased longevity that medical science has gifted to us, you'll find yourself slowing down and more aware of your limitations. This is the stage where health issues might start to crop up. Health care expenses are a growing concern for today's retirees, and you will want to have a conversation with your professional advisor about how to plan for these expenses.

According to a 2013 Fidelity Investments study, a 65-year-old couple will need an additional $240,000 of income to pay for medical expenses throughout their retirement, and this figure doesn't include the rising costs of long term care expenses.* The Congressional Budget Office reported in 2004 an annual cost of $66,000 for a private room in a nursing home, but this is a national average—the cost may be higher in your area.** What are the chances that you or your spouse will need long term care? According to the U.S. Department of Health and Human Services, 70 percent of retirees age 65 will need some form of

---

*http://www.aarp.org/health/medicare-insurance/info-12-2012/health-care-costs.html#.
VDxfScqjIF8.email
**http://www.cbo.gov/publication/15584

long term care in their future years, and 20 percent of those cases will require care for five years or more.* A complete approach to income planning during retirement should include a strategy that reviews and examines possible funding choices to cover the need for increased health costs and the possibility of long term care. Medicare is a government-funded program available to retirees over the age of 65, but it is not designed to cover prolonged stays at nursing homes. For long term care due to chronic illness, today's retirees have more choices and funding options, such as insurance products that provide Living Benefits and annuities with critical care riders. With these products, including long term care expense in your retirement roadmap means the money is there if you need it, but if you don't need it, the funds are simply transferred to your beneficiaries.

HOPE AND A PRAYER PLAN VS HIGH PROBABILITY OF SUCCESS PLAN

Once we have a clear understanding of your goals, the next step is to take a look at where you are at with regard to your finances. This involves taking an inventory of all of your assets, savings, and investments. In order to create a sustainable retirement income plan, your financial professional will look at your retirement plans, mutual funds, annuities, insurance, stocks and bonds and a host of other assets. These investments will then be analyzed in terms of their risk and whether or not they are in support of your short and long term goals.

Before the reports are run, your ability to know whether or not these investments can support you is based on hopes, feelings and prayers. Once the analysis is complete, you can then choose investments based on their ability to provide you with what you need during retirement: income, tax diversification, health care

---

*http://longtermcare.gov/the-basics/how-much-care-will-you-need/

provisions, and legacy. This will turn your hope and a prayer plan into a plan with a high probability of success.

Let's begin by taking a look at some of the basic truths about money as it relates to saving for retirement. There are essentially two kinds of money: **Hope So** and **Know So**. Everyone can divide their money into these two categories. Some have more of one kind than the other. The goal isn't to eliminate one kind of money but to balance them as you approach retirement.

Hope So Money, or Red money, is money that is at risk. It fluctuates with the market. It has no minimum guarantee. It is subject to investor activity, stock prices, market trends, buying trends, etc. You get the picture. This money is exposed to more risk but also has the potential for more reward. Because the market is subject to change, you can't really be sure what the value of your investments will be worth in the future. You can't really *rely* on it at all. For this reason, we refer to it as *Hope So* Money. This doesn't mean you shouldn't have some money invested in the market, but it would be dangerous to assume you can know what it will be worth in the future.

Hope So Money is an important element of a retirement plan, especially in the early stages of planning when you can trade volatility for potential returns, and when a longer investment timeframe is available to you. In the long run, time can smooth out the ups and downs of money exposed to the market. Working with a professional and leveraging a long-term investment strategy has the potential to create rewarding returns from *Hope So* Money.

Know So Money, or Green money, on the other hand, is safer when compared to *Hope So* Money. *Know So* Money is made up of dependable, low-risk or no-risk money, and investments that you can count on. Social Security is one of the most common forms of *Know So* Money. Income you draw or will draw from Social Security is guaranteed. You have paid into Social Security your entire career, and you can rely on that money during your retirement. Unlike the market, rates of growth for *Know So* Money are dependent on 10-year treasury rates. The 10-year treasury, or TNX, is commonly considered to represent a very secure and safe place for your money, hence *Know So* Money. The 10-year treasury drives key rates for things such as mortgages or CDs. *Know So* Money may not be as exciting as *Hope So* Money, but it is safer. You can safely be fairly sure you will have it in the future.

Knowing the difference between *Hope So* and *Know So* Money is an important step towards a successful retirement plan. People who are 55 or older and who are looking ahead to retirement should be relying on more *Know So* Money than *Hope So* Money.

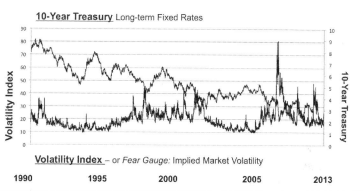

10-Year Treasury Long-term Fixed Rates

Volatility Index – or *Fear Gauge:* Implied Market Volatility

1990   1995   2000   2005   2013

Source: Yahoo Finance 12-31-2013. VIX is a trademarked ticker symbol for the Chicago Board Options Exchange Market Volatility Index, a popular measure of the implied volatility of S&P 500 index options. Often referred to as the fear index or the fear gauge, it represents one measure of the market's expectation of stock market volatility over the next 30 day period. (wikipedia.com) The CBOE 10-year Treasury Note (TNX) is based on 10 times the yield-to-maturity on the most recently auctioned 10-year Treasury note. Past performance does not guarantee future results. Some illustrations may show how a market index has performed. An investor cannot invest in an index, although there are some investments designed to mirror index performance. Past performance is not a guarantee of future results.

The VIX, or volatility index, of the market represents expected market volatility. When the VIX drops, economic experts expect less volatility. When the VIX rises, more volatility is expected.

1. *VIX is a trademarked ticker symbol for the Chicago Board Options Exchange (CBOE) Market Volatility Index, a popular measure of the implied volatility of S&P 500 index options. Often referred to as the fear index or the fear gauge, it represents one measure of the market's expectation of stock market volatility over the next 30 day period. (wikipedia.com)*

2. *The CBOE 10-Year Treasury Note (TNX) is based on 10 times the yield-to-maturity on the most recently auctioned 10-year Treasury note.*

Ideally, the rates of return on *Hope So* and *Know So* Money would have an overlapping area that provided an acceptable rate of risk for both types of money. In the early 1990s, interest rates were high and market volatility was low. At that time, you could invest in either *Hope So* or *Know So* Money options because the rates of return were similar from both *Know So* and *Hope So* investments, and you were likely to be fairly successful with a wide range of investment options. At that time, you could expose yourself to an acceptable amount of risk or an acceptable fixed rate. Basically, it was difficult to make a mistake during that time period. Today, you don't have those options. Market volatility is at all-time highs while interest rates are at all-time lows. They are so far apart from each other that it is hard to know what to do with your money.

Yesterday's investment rules may not work today. Not only could they hamper achieving your goals, they may actually harm your financial situation. We are currently in a period when the rates for *Know So* Money options are at historic lows, and the volatility of *Hope So* Money is higher than ever. There is no overlapping acceptable rate, making both options less than ideal. *Because of this uncertain financial landscape, wise investment strategies are more important now than ever.*

This unique situation requires fresh ideas and investment tools that haven't been relied on in the past. Investing the way your parents did will not pay off. The majority of investment ideas used by financial professionals in the 1990s aren't applicable to today's markets. That kind of investing will likely get you in trouble and compromise your retirement. Today, you need a better PLAN.

HOW MUCH RISK ARE YOU EXPOSED TO?

Many investors don't know how much risk they are exposed to. It is helpful to organize your assets so you can have a clear understanding of how much of your money is at risk and how much is in safer holdings. This process starts with listing all your assets. Let's take a look at the two kinds of money:

Hope So Money is, as the name indicates, money that you *hope* will be there when you need it. *Hope So* Money represents what you would like to get out of your investments. Examples of *Hope So* Money include:
- Stock market funds, including index funds
- Mutual funds
- Variable annuities
- REITS

Know So Money is money that you know you can count on. It is safer money that isn't exposed to the level of volatility as the asset types noted above. You can more confidently count on having this money when you need it. Examples of *Know So* Money are:
- Government backed bonds
- Savings and checking accounts
- Fixed income annuities
- CDs
- Treasuries
- Money market accounts

> » *Vincent had a modest brokerage account that he added to when he could. When he changed jobs a couple years ago, at age 58, Vincent transferred his 401(k) assets into an IRA. Just a few years from retirement, he is now beginning to realize that nearly every dollar he has saved for retirement is subject to market risk.*
>
> *Intuitively, he knows that the time has come to shift some assets to an alternative that is safer, but how much is the right amount?*

THE RULE OF 100

Determining the amount of risk that is right for you is dependent on a number of variables. You need to feel comfortable with where and how you are investing your money, and your financial professional is obligated to help you make decisions that put your money in places that fit your risk criteria.

Your retirement needs to first accommodate your day-to-day income needs. How much money do you need to maintain your lifestyle? When do you need that money? While there is no single approach to investment risk that is universally applicable to everyone, there are some helpful guidelines. One of the most useful is called *The Rule of 100*.

The average investor needs to accumulate assets to create a retirement plan that provides income during retirement and also allows for legacy planning. To accomplish this, they need to balance the amount of risk to which they are exposed. Risk is required because, while *Know So* Money is safer, more reliable and more dependable, it doesn't grow very fast, if at all. Today's historically low interest rates barely break even with current inflation. *Hope So* Money, while less dependable, has more potential for growth. *Hope So* Money can eventually become *Know So* Money once you move it to an investment with lower risk. Everyone's risk diversification will be different depending on their goals, age and their existing assets.

So how do you decide how much risk your assets should be exposed to? Where do you begin? Luckily, there's a guideline you can use to start making decisions about risk management. It's called the Rule of 100.

CALCULATING YOUR RISK NUMBER

The Rule of 100 is a general rule that helps shape asset diversification* for the average investor. The rule states that the number 100 minus an investor's age equals the amount of assets they should have exposed to risk.

The Rule of 100: 100 - (your age) = the percentage of your assets that should be exposed to risk (*Hope So* Money)

For example, if you are a 30-year-old investor, the Rule of 100 would indicate that you should be focusing on investing primarily in the market and taking on a substantial amount of risk in your portfolio. The Rule of 100 suggests that 70 percent of your investments should be exposed to risk.

100 - (30 years of age) = 70 percent

Now, not every 30-year-old should have exactly 70 percent of their assets in mutual funds and stocks. The Rule of 100 is based on your chronological age, not your "financial age," which could vary based on your investment experience, your aversion or acceptance

Asset Diversification disclosure – Diversification and asset allocation does not assure or guarantee better performance and cannot eliminate the risk of investment loss. Before investing, you should carefully read the applicable volatility disclosure for each of the underlying funds, which can be found in the current prospectus.

of risk and other factors. While this rule isn't an ironclad solution to anyone's finances, it's a pretty good place to start. Once you've taken the time to look at your assets with a professional advisor to determine your risk exposure, you can use the Rule of 100 to make changes that put you in a more stable investment position; one that reflects your comfort level.

Perhaps when you were age 30 and starting your career (as in the example above) it would make sense to have 70 percent of your money in the market: you have time on your side. You have plenty of time to save more money, work more, and recover from a downturn in the market. Retirement was ages away, and your earning power was increasing. And indeed, younger investors should take on more risk for exactly those reasons. The potential reward of long-term involvement in the market outweighs the risk of investing when you are young.

Risk tolerance generally reduces as you get older. However, if you are 40 years old and lose 30 percent of your portfolio in a market downturn this year, you have 20 or 30 years to recover it. If you are 68 years old, you only have 5 to 10 years (or less) to make the same recovery. That new circumstance changes your whole retirement perspective. At age 68, it's likely that you simply aren't as interested in suffering through a tough stock market. There is less time to recover from downturns and the stakes are much higher. The money you have saved is money you will soon need to provide you with income, or even money that you already need to meet your income demands.

Much of the flexibility that comes with investing earlier in life is related to *compounding*. Compounded earnings can be incredibly powerful over time. The longer your money has time to compound, the greater your wealth will be. This is what most people refer to as *"putting their money to work."* This is also why the Rule of 100 favors risk for the young. If you start investing when you are young, you can invest smaller amounts of money in a more aggressive fashion because you have the potential to make a profit in a rising market and you can harness the power of compounding earnings. When you are 40, 50, or 60 years old, that potential becomes less and less. You are forced to have more money at lower amounts of risk to realize the same returns. **It basically becomes more expensive to prudently invest the older you get.**

You risk not having a recovery period the older you get, so you should have less of your assets at risk in volatile investments. You should shift with the Rule of 100 to protect your assets and ensure that they will provide you with the income you need in retirement. Let's look at another example that illustrates how the Rule of 100 becomes more critical as you age. For example, an 80-year-old investor who is retired and is relying on retirement assets for income, needs to depend on a solid amount of *Know So Money*. The Rule of 100 says an 80-year-old investor should have a maximum of 20 percent of his or her assets at risk. Depending on the investor's financial position, even less risk exposure may be required. You are the only person who can make this kind of determination. Although, the Rule of 100 can help, everyone has their own level of comfort. Your Rule of 100 results will be based on your values, attitudes, as well as your comfort with risk. A financial professional can look at your assets with you and discuss alternatives to optimize your balance between *Know So* and *Hope So* Money.

CHAPTER 1 CHECKLIST //

- Have you identified what you want to be doing during your retirement? Do you know when you will stop working, what activities you will be enjoying, and who you will be sharing adventures with?
- Do you understand the difference between professionals held to fiduciary standards of liability and those held to suitability standards? Do you trust the financial professional in charge of designing your comprehensive retirement plan?
- Have you identified foreseeable financial challenges and made plans for all three stages of retirement: Go-Go, Go-Slow and No-Go?
- Do you understand where and how your assets are currently invested in terms of *Hope So* and *Know So* investments?
- Have you used the Rule of 100 as a general guiding principle to determine how much risk your retirement investments should be exposed to? (100 - [your age] = [percentage of your investments that can comfortably have exposed to risk]).

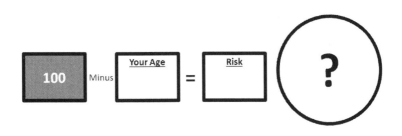

2

DO YOU HAVE THE RIGHT INVESTMENTS FOR YOU?

"It ain't what you don't know that gets you into trouble.
It's what you know for sure that just ain't so."
– Mark Twain

Don is 59 years old and Amy is 57 years old. They both plan on working for another 5 to 8 years. They want to continue investing in their company 401(k) plan in order to get the employer contributions and tax benefits. However, when looking at their investments in terms of Hope So and Know So Money, Don and Amy realize they are exposed to far more risk than they thought. Their 401(k) plan is invested 100 percent in Hope So investments, yet according to the Rule of 100, they should both be transitioning at least 50 percent of their funds into more secure, Know So investments.

Their financial professional shows them one way they can take more control over their 401(k) accounts. Most people don't realize that even when they are still working, the majority of employee benefit plans allow for something called an in-service withdrawal at age 59 1/2. This gives plan participants like Don and Amy the ability to roll a percentage of their 401(k) holdings out of the stock market and into an IRA where they will have access to more investment options. From there, they can choose among a multitude of safer investments. Meanwhile, they can still contribute to their 401(k) and get the employer matches. Now, Don and Amy are much more comfortable knowing that the majority of their retirement savings are safe and not subject to market volatility.

A lot of investors like Don and Amy know a lot less about the actual risk their investments are really exposed to. They think they have safe investments because their 401(k) is composed of mutual funds, or they assume their broker dealer is giving them good advice. Most people rely heavily on mutual funds during the accumulation phase of life. Your company 401(k) plan might have offered a selection of mutual funds to choose from, and at the time you made what you thought were the best choices. The question is, are these still the best investments now, prior to and during retirement?

DO YOU KNOW WHAT YOU OWN?

During the Great Recession of 2008, a lot of investors watched with horror as their investment portfolios were cut by 30 percent or more. Employees like Don and Amy who were nearing retirement were faced with some serious decisions as to whether or not they could retire as planned. How long would their savings last them once they started making withdrawals? Most 401(k) plans don't provide a place to hide during market volatility, which is why many employee plans now offer an in-service withdrawal option. Instead of waiting until age 59 ½, federal law now allows the vast majority of employees in 401(k) plans the ability to take control of their assets while still working, effectively shifting a portion of your assets into safer, more secure options.

How much risk are your investments exposed to? Is that risk quantified by an appropriate amount of reward? Are your investments balanced to provide an income that can support you during the long journey ahead?

Finding the right investment tool for the job during today's volatile economy often means utilizing more than one type of investment, which is why many professionals held to fiduciary standards rely on in-depth reports and tests in order to get an objective view of your current holdings. The Morningstar Report uses a sophisticated computer algorithm program to assess how your assets are currently allocated and how their performance compares with other indices in terms of both return and yield. The Yahoo Finance site on the Internet is one place anyone can go to when searching for a way to quantify an investment's risk and reward. Your financial professional might also do a Risk Reward Analysis that drills down even deeper to find out the true amount of risk your investments are exposed to.

STRESS-TEST YOUR INVESTMENTS

Imagine your investment portfolio is in the hospital, connected to an EKG reading. What would the heart-line monitor readings on your investments look like? Would they be zig-zagging? Are there alarms beeping? Would that reading put you on your financial death bed? While this is said tongue-in-cheek, using a sophisticated computer analysis reports such as the Retirement Income Analysis allows you to play the "what if" game so you can stress-test your investments and see how they would perform under pressure. What would happen to your retirement income if your spouse passed away? What would happen to your retirement income if you got a chronic illness? What will happen to the security of your retirement income when the stock market takes another downturn like the one in 2008?

Notice in the above sentence it reads **when** the stock market takes another downturn and not **if**. Since 1900, we've had 22 recessions in this country. That's one major market downturn every 5 to 6 years. If you're 65 years old today, this mean you may see another 5 to 6 recessions during your lifetime. With regard to market downturns and your retirement savings, how many -20 percent years can you take? How many -30 percent years can you take? How many -40 percent years? Most people know they can **NOT** afford any and that's a perfectly acceptable assessment. Why should you have to lose any of your hard-earned money? The problem is, most people have no idea what investments they own or how those investments will perform under certain market conditions. Playing the *"what if"* game gives you the opportunity to step back and look at the bigger picture.

At the end of the day, what these risks really boil down to is whether or not you'll be able to maintain the standard of living you've grown accustomed to for the duration of your retirement. To explain the risk inherent in your investments, it can be helpful to organize your assets into a visual schematic.

THE COLORS OF MONEY

Over the many years of your lifetime, it is likely that you have acquired a variety of assets. Assets can range from money that you have in a savings account or a 401(k), to a pension or an IRA. You have earned money and have made financial decisions based on the best information you had at the time. When viewed as a whole, however, you might not have an overall strategy for the management of your assets. As we have seen, it's more important than ever to know which of your assets are at risk. High market volatility and low treasury rates make for challenging financial topography. Navigating this financial landscape starts with planful asset management that takes into account your specific goals.

Visually organizing your assets is an important and powerful way to get a clear picture of what kind of money you have, where it is and how you can best use it in the future. Even if you feel that you have plenty of money in your 401(k) or IRA, not knowing how much *risk* those investments are exposed to can cause you major financial suffering. The colors red, green, yellow and orange can be used to identify the different levels of risk your money is exposed to according the investment type. The way you organize your assets depends on your goals and your level of comfort with risk. For our purposes, *Know So* Money (which is safer and more dependable) is green. *Hope So* Money (which is exposed to risk and fluctuates with the market) is red.

Some retirees today find that with the current economy and market volatility, a little more color is needed to balance out their portfolios. Yellow Money is Red Money that is being professionally managed in a conservative growth portfolio. Orange Money is Red Money that is being managed in a moderate growth portfolio. Yellow and Orange Money portfolios have risk associated with them, but because this money is under the watchful eye of a professional, that risk is mitigated. The professional managing your money should know not just about the investments, but about you—what you need the money for and how you expect the investment to perform.

Some financial firms apply strict benchmark criteria when choosing money managers for client portfolios. For example, they must have a track record of at least 10 years, with a proven average of at least 7 percent. A money manager with a six year track record would not be eligible. This ten-year benchmark allows the firm to see how the money manager performed during market recessions such as those experienced during the years 2001 and 2008. A second criteria required may be for the money manager to have either stayed flat or made a profit during those same bad years, including years 2000, 2001, 2002 and 2008.

The next step is to know the right amount and ratio of Green, Yellow and Orange Money for you at your stage of retirement planning. Investing heavily in Red Money and gambling all of your assets on the market is incredibly risky no matter where you fall within the Rule of 100. Money in the market can't be depended on to generate income. A plan that leans too heavily on Red Money can easily fail, especially when investment decisions are influenced by emotional reactions to market downturns and recoveries. Not only is this an unwise plan, it can be incredibly stressful to an investor who is gambling everything on stocks and mutual funds.

But a plan that uses too much Green Money avoids all volatility and can also fail. Why? Investing all of your money in Certificates of Deposit (CDs), savings accounts, money markets and other low return accounts may provide interest and income, but likely won't be enough to keep pace with inflation. If you focus exclusively on income from Green Money and avoid owning any stocks or mutual funds in your portfolio, you won't be able to leverage the potential for long-term growth your portfolio needs to stay healthy and productive. This is where the Rule of 100 can help you determine how much of your money should be invested in the market to anticipate your future needs.

Green Money becomes much more important as you age. While you want to reduce the amount of Red Money you have and transition it to Green Money, you don't necessarily need all of it to generate income for you right away. Which is where your Yellow and Orange Money investments can come into play.

BUCKET FINANCING

Once we've identified your retirement goals and current investment risk, it's time to start taking a look how we can better position those assets in order to achieve those goals. The Bucket System can be a helpful way to organize your assets according to what the money will be used for and the risk inherent in those investments. Colors can be associated with each bucket to indicate the inherent risk in those investments. Bucket A can be thought of as Green, Bucket B can be Yellow and Bucket C can be Orange. You, the investor, get to choose what percentage of your funds will be allocated to each bucket and for how long. Having multiple buckets set for different needs and growth durations ensures that the money you need for income will be available when you need it.

Bucket A: GREEN MONEY: These investments are safe and secure—you cannot lose your principal and you cannot lose your gains with the money in your Green Bucket. You can realistically expect to average 5, 6 and maybe 7 percent each year over the course of 5-10-15-20 years plus. These are NET returns after the calculations of fees and expenses. This bucket is set for long term consistency. These investments can provide you with a guaranteed income for life if that is what you want to do. What percentage of your assets would you allocate to this bucket?

Bucket B: YELLOW MONEY: Although Yellow Money investments are not guaranteed, they offer lower risk and lower volatility with a much higher probability for success than using the *"Hope and a Prayer"* model of *Hope So* Money investments. Yellow Money investments are under the watchful eye of a professional and most of the private wealth managers used by fiduciary firms have 70 to 80 percent less risk than national the stock market averages. You can realistically expect to achieve average returns of 6, 7, and maybe 8 percent per year in a net profit after fees and expenses for the next 5-10-15-20 years plus. This is money you can grow for later income needs to be used during the Go-Slow or

RETIREMENT DESIGNED MANAGEMENT SYSTEM
3 Bucket Risk Management

GUARANTEED Safe & Secure	Low Risk/Low Volatility Investment	Moderate Risk Investment
A ____%	**B** ____%	**C** ____%
Goal 5-7% per year 5-10-15- 20 years	Goal 6-8% per year 5-10-15-20 years	Goal 9-11% per year 5-10-15-20 years

No-Go phases of your retirement journey. What percent of your assets would you allocate to this bucket?

Bucket C: ORANGE MONEY: These investments are not guaranteed safe and secured, but neither are they high risk. Orange Money is considered moderate risk. Private wealth managers with proven track records can usually achieve returns as high as 9, 10, and maybe 11 percent with 60 percent less risk than average stock market returns as compared to investors going it alone. This is money set for growth for 5-10-15-20 years down the road to be used for the later phases of your retirement journey. Orange Money managers have "sell discipline," which means they are not afraid to take your money out of the market during volatile times. What percent of your assets would you like in this bucket?

The amount of money you have saved matters, but what you do or don't do with that money matters even more. You might have a million dollars socked away in a savings account, but your neighbor who has $300,000 as part of a cohesive plan with maximized efficiencies to provide sustainable income and an increase net worth will most likely enjoy a better retirement lifestyle. Why? Your neighbor had more than a good work ethic and a penchant for saving. They had a plan that incorporated all the pieces of the retirement puzzle.

THE NUMBERS DON'T LIE

When the rubber meets the road, the numbers dictate your options. Your risk tolerance is an important indicator of what kinds of investments you should consider, but if the returns from those investments don't meet your retirement goals, your income needs will likely not be met. For example, if the level of risk you are comfortable with manages your investments at a 4 percent return and you need to realize an 8 percent return, your income needs aren't going to be met when you need to rely on your investments for retirement income. A professional may encourage you to be more aggressive with your investment strategy by taking on more risk in order to give you the potential of earning a greater return. If taking more risk isn't an option that you are comfortable with, then the discussion will turn to how you can earn more money or spend less in order to align your needs with your resources more closely.

How are you going to structure your income flow during retirement? The answer to this question dictates how you determine your risk tolerance. If the numbers say that you need to be more aggressive with your investing, or that you need to modify your lifestyle, it becomes a choice you need to make.

12 RISKS THAT COULD GET YOU OFF TRACK

Aside from stock market risk, there are other risk factors that have the ability to cast asunder the best laid plans. We aim to protect against as many of these risks as possible.

On a journey of this magnitude, chances are you'll encounter more than one or two bumps in the road such as an increase in taxes or chronic illness. Will you be prepared? We don't know what risk will have the biggest impact on your specific situation or in what order these risks will come, but we want you to be prepared. Consider the following 12 risks now, during the planning phase, so they won't throw you off track. Instead, you'll have a set detour in place that allows you to navigate the bump or pothole with ease.

1. **Longevity Risk:** Can your income sustain you? Will it last as long as you do?

2. **Entitlement Risk:** Will government programs such as Social Security and Medicare change? Can you count on them to provide sufficient income?

3. **Excess Withdrawal Risk:** Are you drawing down your assets too quickly?

4. **Market Risk:** What would happen to your income if you lost your retirement assets—either temporarily or permanently—due to market downturn or poor investment performance?

5. **Lifestyle Risk:** Will there be sufficient income to maintain your current or expected standard of living?

6. **Asset Allocation Risk:** Are you investing too conservatively or too aggressively? Are your assets properly diversified?

7. **Sequence of Returns:** Will you be lucky enough to receive good rates of return during the early years of your retirement? Low or negative returns during the beginning of your distribution years can significantly diminish your portfolio.

8. **Inflation Risk:** Will rising costs undermine the purchasing power of your retirement assets?

9. **Medical Expense Risk:** Can you afford the growing cost of health care related services during your retirement?

10. **Tax Risk:** What affect can unforeseen tax consequences have on your portfolio or overall purchasing power?

11. **Personal or Event Risk:** What would happen to your income if something happened to you or your spouse? How could a change in your family situation undermine your retirement plans?

12. **Incapacity Risk:** If your health deteriorates, how will you execute sound judgment in managing your retirement affairs?

Consulting with a financial professional is often the wisest approach to addressing risk. A professional can also help determine your risk tolerance by getting to know you, asking you a set of questions and even giving you a survey to determine your comfort level with different types of risk.

What will you be doing during your retirement years? Traveling to Ireland? Starting a new business? Zip-lining through the canopies of Costa Rica? Understanding what you are invested in and preparing for all the risks that come with the challenges of retiring today will help you get you ready for the next step on the retirement readiness checklist: calculating your retirement expenses.

CHAPTER 2 CHECKLIST //

- Do you understand the different features and distribution options of your employer-sponsored retirement plans?
- Have you increased your savings by investing the maximum into your 401(k) and IRAs before leaving the workforce?
- Have you reviewed your portfolio to make sure your investments still reflect your goals and feelings about risk? Have you stress-tested your investments to see how they would perform under certain *what if* scenarios?
- Do you understand what you are invested in and why? Have you organized your assets according to color: Green Money assets that are "safer" and more reliable; Red Money assets that represent high exposure to risk?
- Are you working with a financial professional to find appropriate Green, Yellow and maybe even Orange Money options for your situation?
- Have you evaluated how changes in the economy will affect your pension, investments and retirement benefits? Do you know the amount you can withdraw from your nest egg each year so you won't run out of money?
- Do you understand the financial risks that can impact the stability of your retirement income: longer lifespan, inflation, conservative investing, aggressive withdrawals, market risk and health care expenses?

3

CREATING AN INCOME
FOR LIFE

Guessing is not an income strategy.

Finding the most efficient and beneficial way to address your income needs impacts lifestyle, asset accumulation and legacy planning. The moment your working income ceases and you start living off the money you've set aside for retirement is referred to as the retirement cliff. When you begin drawing income from your retirement assets, you have entered the distribution phase of your financial plan. **The distribution phase of your retirement plan** is when you reach the point of relying on your assets for income. This is where your Green Money comes into play: the safer, more reliable assets that you have accumulated that are designed to provide you with a steady income. On day one of your retirement, you will need a steady and reliable supply of income from your

Green Money. You may also want a strategic Yellow or Orange Money growth portfolio in place to plan for your income needs down the road. Satisfying the need for daily income entails first knowing *how much you need* and *when you will need it.*

WHAT LIFESTYLE DO YOU WANT TO MAINTAIN?

Think about your current lifestyle and imagine what it would take to maintain that lifestyle 5 or 10 years down the road. Is your house paid off? Do you have credit card debt? Is it time to downsize in order to cut expenses? *Every financial strategy for retirement needs first to accommodate the day-to-day need for income.* Imagining what you want your day-to-day life to look like is one way to help shed light on lifestyle choices that have to be made as you enter this new phase. If you are 5 or more years away from retirement, your income plan might include a way to retire your debt so those expenses don't hinder the lifestyle you want to maintain once you stop working. You may also want to consider the possibility of eliminating one your vehicles to cut insurance and car maintenance bills.

As you calculate what your expenses in retirement will be, keep in mind that some expenses will increase while others may decrease or disappear altogether. Consistent expenses usually include the following:
- Food and clothing
- Housing
- Taxes
- Utilities (gas and electric)
- Transportation (including fuel, car insurance and repairs)
- Health Care

Expenses which fluctuate and which you have more control over include some of the more adventurous things you might see yourself doing during the Go-Go phase of your retirement. These expenses can include the following:

- Travel
- Entertainment
- Recreation

While most retirees can expect to see an increase in health care expenses, there may also be a decrease in some of these consistent expenses. Statistics from the U.S. Department of Labor on consumer expenditures reveals that retirement spending doesn't stay level throughout the years. The early phase of retirement, or the Go-Go phase, is when expenditures are at their greatest, especially if you factor in travel. Overall living expenses for items such as consumer durables, transportation and even food are also likely to decline during the Go-Slow and No-Go phase.

How much money will you need to maintain your lifestyle during retirement? While this amount will be different for everyone, the general rule of thumb is that a retiree will require 70 to 80 percent of their pre-retirement income to maintain their lifestyle. Once you know what that number is, the key becomes matching your income need with the correct investment strategies, options and tools to satisfy that need.

WHEN DO YOU NEED IT?

While none of us knows for certain how many years we have left to live, there are some variables we have control over when it comes to the expected duration of our retirement income. Those variables include when and how you plan to retire.

- Do you plan to work part-time for a few years?
- Will you be starting a business?
- Are there certain expenses you expect to crop up in the future such as health care costs?

- Are you aware that your IRA will require that you begin making withdrawals at the age of 70 ½?
- Are you expecting to sell some real estate property?
- Will you be inheriting any money?

Creating an income plan that lasts as long as you do requires careful planning for all your income needs 10, 15, and sometimes even 30 years down the road.

If you need your income to last you 10 years, you will want to use an investment tool or combination of tools that creates just that. If you would feel more secure knowing you have a guaranteed source of lifetime income, seek Green Money investments that can provide you with safe money guarantees. If health care costs, potential emergencies and plans for traveling require that your investments have a strong growth component, then talk to your financial professional about Yellow and Orange Money portfolio options.

While you want to reduce the amount of *Hope So* Money you have and transition it to *Know So* Money, you don't necessarily need all of it to generate income for you right away. As mentioned earlier, this is where your different buckets of money can come into play. You want to maximize retirement benefits to meet **your lifetime** income needs. A financial professional can help you answer those questions by working with you to customize an income that lasts as long as you do.

WHERE DOES YOUR INCOME COME FROM?

Approaching retirement, you will likely have a patchwork quilt of several income sources from areas such as Social Security, retirement accounts, stocks, bonds and mutual funds, CDs, inheritance, annuities, and money market funds for starters. You might also be lucky enough to be receiving some kind of pension, or you may have income coming from other sources such as real estate rental income or book royalties. The previous steps will help you determine whether you have a projected retirement surplus or a shortfall, known as *the income gap*.

The first place we look for income producing sources are Green Money options such as pensions and Social Security. The amount of income provided by those sources can't be changed, and they provide the retirement base from which you build up from until you reach the number you need. We'll total up your income from all projected sources during retirement that may include the following:

- Income from a pension.
- Income from royalty checks.
- Rental income from apartment buildings, homes, or land rights.
- Wages from a part time job or cottage industry.
- Benefits from Social Security.
- Dividend checks or other investments such as mineral rights.
- Other sources of reliable, guaranteed income.

A *Registered Investment Advisor* can help you customize an income plan based on your current expenses and projected future needs by utilizing a strategy that provides ample income for all the phases of your retirement, from the Go-Go to the No-Go.

One kind of Green Money that most Americans can rely on for income when they retire is Social Security. If you're like most Americans, Social Security is or will be an important part of your retirement income and one that you should know how to properly manage. As a first step in creating your income plan, a financial professional will take a look at your Social Security benefit options. Social Security is the foundation of income planning for anyone who is about to retire today and is such a reliable source of Green Money in your overall income plan, we have dedicated the next chapter in this book to this one subject alone.

CHAPTER 3 CHECKLIST //

- Do you know how much income you will need in retirement to maintain the same standard of living you have now?
- Have you detailed a list of expenses you expect to incur in retirement? Does that list include credit card debt or a mortgage?
- Have you evaluated the impact of debt as you head into retirement? Do you have a plan to pay down your debt or pay off your mortgage? Have you considered downsizing to a smaller house or condo to generate extra income and reduce expenses?
- Have you looked at what your life expectancy could be and do you understand why you may need to plan for 30 years or more of retirement income?
- Have you identified which expenses may increase during retirement and which expenses may decrease? As a general rule, the older one gets, the less one spends, aside from health care costs.
- Do you have sufficient income to service any debt you might have during retirement?
- Have you factored in a cost of living increase into your retirement income needs that takes into account inflationary factors that may affect your purchasing power 10 to 30 years down the road?
- Have you calculated how much income you'll receive during retirement from all available sources? Is that income enough to account for 70 to 80 percent of your current needs? Do you have an income shortfall, or gap, that needs to be funded?

4

UNDERSTANDING
SOCIAL SECURITY

One kind of Green Money that most Americans can rely on for income when they retire is Social Security. If you're like most Americans, Social Security is or will be an important part of your retirement income and one that you should know how to properly manage. As a first step in creating your income plan, a financial professional will take a look at your Social Security benefit options. Social Security is the foundation of income planning for anyone who is about to retire and is a reliable source of Green Money in your overall income plan.

> » *Mary had worked full-time nearly her entire adult life and was looking forward to enjoying retirement with her hus-*

band, kids and grandkids. When she turned 62, she decided to take advantage of her Social Security benefits as soon as they became available.

A couple of years later, she was organizing some of the paperwork in her home office. She came across an old Social Security statement, and remembered the feeling of filing and beginning a new phase in her life.

However, as she looked over the statement, she realized in retrospect that she might have been better off waiting to file for benefits. She had saved enough to wait for benefits, and if she had, her monthly benefit could have been quite a bit more.

When she was in the process of retiring, there were so many other decisions to make. It seemed very straightforward to file right away. She made a note to call the Social Security Administration to see if it was possible to change her monthly benefit to the larger amount.

Here are some facts that illustrate how Americans currently use Social Security:

- Nearly 90 percent of Americans age 65 and older receive Social Security benefits.[*]
- Social Security provides about 39 percent of the income of the elderly.[*]
- Claiming Social Security benefits at the wrong time can reduce your monthly benefit by up to 65 percent.[**]
- In 2013, 36 percent of men and 40 percent of women claimed Social Security benefits at age 62.[***]

---

[*] *https://www.ssa.gov/pressoffice/basicfact.html*

[**] *https://www.ssa.gov/planners/retire/retirechart.html*

[***] *Trends in Social Security Claiming, Alicia H Munnell and Anqi Chen, Center for Retirement Research, May 2015. http://crr.bc.edu/wp-content/uploads/2015/05/*

- In 2013, more than a third of workers claimed Social Security benefits as soon they became eligible.*
- In 2015, the average monthly Social Security benefit was $1,328. The maximum benefit for 2015 was $2,663. The $1,335 monthly benefit reduction between the average and the maximum is applied for life.**

There are many aspects of Social Security that are well known and others that aren't. When it comes time for you to cash in on your Social Security benefit, you will have many options and choices. Social Security is a massive government program that manages retirement benefits for millions of people. Experts spend their entire careers understanding and analyzing it. Luckily, you don't have to understand all of the intricacies of Social Security to maximize its advantages. You simply need to know the best way to manage your Social Security benefit. You need to know exactly what to do to get the most from your Social Security benefit and when to do it. Taking the time to create a roadmap for your Social Security strategy will help ensure that you are able to exact your maximum benefit and efficiently coordinate it with the rest of your retirement plan.

There are many aspects of Social Security that you have no control over. You don't control how much you put into it, and you don't control what it's invested in or how the government manages it. However, you do control when and how you file for benefits. The real question about Social Security that you need to answer is, "When should I start taking Social Security?" While

---

IB_15-8.pdf

* *Trends in Social Security Claiming, Alicia H Munnell and Anqi Chen, Center for Retirement Research, May 2015. http://crr.bc.edu/wp-content/uploads/2015/05/ IB_15-8.pdf*

** *https://www.ssa.gov/news/press/factsheets/colafacts2015.html*

this is the all-important question, there are a couple of key pieces of information you need to track down first.

Before we get into a few calculations and strategies that can make all the difference, let's start by covering the basic information about Social Security which should give you an idea of where you stand. Just as the foundation of a house creates the stable platform for the rest of the framework to rest upon, your Social Security benefit is an important part of your overall retirement plan. The purpose of the information that follows is not to give an exhaustive explanation of how Social Security works, but to give you some tools and questions to start understanding how Social Security affects your retirement and how you can prepare for it.

Let's start with eligibility.

Eligibility. Understanding how and when you are eligible for Social Security benefits will help clarify what to expect when the time comes to claim them.

To receive retirement benefits from Social Security, you must earn eligibility. In almost all cases, Americans born after 1929 must earn 40 quarters of credit to be eligible to draw their Social Security retirement benefit. In 2015, a Social Security credit represents $1,220 earned in a calendar quarter. The number changes as it is indexed each year, but not drastically. In 2014, a credit represented $1,200. Four quarters of credit is the maximum number that can be earned each year. In 2015, an American would have had to earn at least $4,880 to accumulate four credits. In order to qualify for retirement benefits, you must have earned a minimum number of credits. Additionally, if you are at least 62 years old and have been married to a recipient of Social Security benefits for at least 12 months, you can choose to receive Spousal Benefits. Although 40 is the minimum number of credits required to begin drawing benefits, it is important to know that once you claim your Social Security benefit, there is no going back. Although there may be cost of living adjustments made, you are locked into that base benefit amount forever.

Primary Insurance Amount. You can think of your Primary Insurance Amount (PIA) like a ripening fruit. It represents the amount of your Social Security benefit at your Full Retirement Age (FRA). Your benefit becomes fully ripe at your FRA, and will neither reduce nor increase due to early or delayed retirement options. If you opt to take benefits before your FRA, however, your monthly benefit will be less than your PIA. You will essentially be picking an unripened fruit. On the one hand, waiting until after your FRA to access your benefits will increase your benefit beyond your PIA. On the other hand, you don't want the fruit to overripen, because every month you wait is one less check you get from the government.

Full Retirement Age. Your FRA is an important figure for anyone who is planning to rely on Social Security benefits in their retirement. Depending on when you were born, there is a specific age at which you will attain FRA. Your FRA is dictated by your year of birth and is the age at which you can begin your full monthly benefit. Your FRA is important because it is half of the equation used to calculate your Social Security benefit. The other half of the equation is based on when you start taking benefits.

When Social Security was initially set up, the FRA was age 65, and it still is for people born before 1938. But as time has passed, the age for receiving full retirement benefits has increased. If you were born between 1938 and 1960, your full retirement age is somewhere on a sliding scale between 65 and 67. Anyone born in 1960 or later will now have to wait until age 67 for full benefits. Increasing the FRA has helped the government reduce the cost of the Social Security program, which paid out almost $870 billion to beneficiaries in 2015!*

---

* *https://www.ssa.gov/news/press/basicfact.html*

While you can begin collecting benefits as early as age 62, the amount you receive as a monthly benefit will be less than it would be if you wait until you reached your FRA or surpass your FRA. It is important to note that if you file for your Social Security benefit before your FRA, *the reduction to your monthly benefit will remain in place for the rest of your life.* You can also delay receiving benefits up to age 70, in which case your benefits will be higher than your PIA for the rest of your life.

- At FRA, 100 percent of PIA is available as a monthly benefit.
- At age 62, your Social Security retirement benefits are available. For each month you take benefits prior to your FRA, however, the monthly amount of your benefit is reduced. *This reduction stays in place for the rest of your life.*
- At age 70, your monthly benefit reaches its maximum. After you turn age 70, your monthly benefit will no longer increase.

Year of Birth	Full Retirement Age
1943-1954	66
1955	66 and 2 months
1956	66 and 4 months
1957	66 and 6 months
1958	66 and 8 months
1959	66 and 10 months
1960 or later	age 67*

---

* *http://www.ssa.gov/OACT/progdata/nra.html*

ROLLING UP YOUR SOCIAL SECURITY

Your Social Security income "rolls up" the longer you wait to claim it. Your monthly benefit will continue to increase until you turn 70 years old. Even though Social Security is the foundation of most people's retirement, many Americans feel that they don't have control over how or when they receive their benefits. The truth is that every dollar you increase your Social Security income by means less money you will have to spend from your nest egg to meet your retirement income needs, but many retirees do not take advantage of this fact. For many people, creating their Social Security strategy is the most important decision they can make to positively impact their retirement. *The difference between the best and worst Social Security decision can be tens of thousands of dollars over a lifetime of benefits.*

Deciding NOW or LATER: Following the above logic, it makes sense to wait as long as you can to begin receiving your Social Security benefit. However, the answer isn't always that simple. Not everyone has the option of waiting. Many people need to rely on Social Security on day one of their retirement. Some might need the income. Others might be in poor health and don't feel they will live long enough to make FRA worthwhile for themselves or their families. It is also possible, however, that the majority of folks taking an early benefit at age 62 are simply under-informed about Social Security. Perhaps they make this major decision based on rumors and emotion.

File Immediately if You:
- Find your job is unbearable.
- Are willing to sacrifice retirement income.
- Are not healthy and need a reliable source of income.

Consider Delaying Your Benefit if You:
- Want to maximize your retirement income.
- Want to increase retirement benefits for your spouse.
- Are still working and like it.
- Are healthy and willing / able to wait to file.

So if you decide to wait, how long should you wait? Lots of people can put it off for a few years, but not everyone can wait until they are 70 years old. Your individual circumstances may be able to help you determine when you should begin taking Social Security. If you do the math, you will quickly see that between ages 62 and 70, there are 96 months in which you can file for your Social Security benefit. If you take into account those 96 months and the 96 months your spouse could also file for Social Security, the number of different strategies for structuring your benefit, you can easily end up with more than 20,000 different scenarios. It's safe to say this isn't the kind of math that most people can easily handle. Each month would result in a different benefit amount. The longer you wait, the higher your monthly benefit amount becomes. Each month you wait, however, is one less month that you receive a Social Security check.

The goal is to maximize your lifetime benefits. That may not always mean waiting until you can get the largest monthly payment. Taking the bigger picture into account, you want to find out how to get the most money out of Social Security over the number of years that you draw from it. Don't underestimate the power of optimizing your benefit: the difference between the BEST and WORST Social Security election can easily be worth thousands of dollars in lifetime benefits. *The difference can be very substantial!*

If you know that every month you wait, your Social Security benefit goes up a little bit, and you also know that every month you wait, you receive one less benefit check, how do you determine where the sweet spot is that maximizes your benefits over your lifetime? Financial professionals have access to software that will calculate the best year and month for you to file for benefits based on your default life expectancy. You can further customize that information by estimating your life expectancy based on your health, habits and family history. If you can then create an income plan (we'll get into this later in the chapter) that helps you wait until the target date for you to file for Social Security, you can optimize your retirement income strategy to get the most out of your Social Security benefit. How can you calculate your life expectancy? Well, you don't know exactly how long you'll live, but you have a better idea than the government does. They rely on averages to make their calculations. ***You have much more personal information about your health, lifestyle and family history than they do.*** You can use that knowledge to game the system and beat all the other people who are making uninformed decisions by filing early for Social Security.

While you can and should educate yourself about how Social Security works, the reality is you don't need to know a lot of general information about Social Security in order to make choices about your retirement. What you do need to know is exactly ***what to do to maximize your benefit.*** Because knowing what you need to do has huge impacts on your retirement! For most Americans, Social Security is the foundation of income planning for retirement. Social Security benefits represent about 39 percent of the income of the elderly.* For many people, it can represent the largest portion of their retirement income. Not treating your Social Security benefit as an asset and investment tool can lead to sub-optimization of your largest source of retirement income.

Let's take a look at an example that shows the impact of working with a financial professional to optimize Social Security benefits:

---

* *https://www.ssa.gov/OACT/progdata/nra.html*

» George and Mary Bailey are a typical American couple who have worked their whole lives and saved when they could. George is 60 years old, and Mary is 56 years old. They sat down with a financial professional who logged onto the Social Security website to look up their PIAs. George's PIA is $1,900 and Mary's is $900.

If the Baileys cash in at age 62 and begin taking retirement benefits from Social Security, they will receive an estimated $568,600 in lifetime benefits. That may seem like a lot, but if you divide that amount over 20 years, it averages out to around $28,400 per year. The Baileys are accustomed to a more significant annual income than that. To make up the difference, they will have to rely on alternative retirement income options. They will basically have to depend on a bigger nest egg to provide them with the income they need.

If they wait until their FRA, they will increase their lifetime benefits to an estimated $609,000. This option allows them to achieve their Primary Insurance Amount, which will provide them a $34,200 annual income.

After learning the Baileys' needs and using software to calculate the most optimal time to begin drawing benefits, the Baileys' financial professional determined that the best option for them drastically increases their potential lifetime benefits to $649,000!

By using strategies that their financial professional recommended, they increased their potential lifetime benefits by as much as $80,000. There's no telling how much you could miss out on from your Social Security if you don't take time to create a strategy that calculates your maximum benefit. For the Baileys, the value of maximizing their benefits was the difference between night and day. While this may seem like a special case, it isn't uncommon to find benefit increases of this *magnitude. You'll never know unless you take a look at your own options.*

Despite the importance of knowing when and how to take your Social Security benefit, many of today's retirees and pre-retirees may know little about the mechanics of Social Security and how they can maximize their benefit.

So, to whom should you turn for advice when making this complex decision? Before you pick up the phone and call Uncle Sam, you should know that the Social Security Administration (SSA) representatives are actually prohibited from giving you election advice! Plus, SSA representatives in general are trained to focus on monthly benefit amounts, not the lifetime income for a family.

MAXIMIZING YOUR LIFETIME BENEFIT

As discussed earlier, calculating how to maximize **lifetime benefits** is more important than waiting until age 70 for your maximum **monthly benefit amount**. It's about getting the most income during your lifetime. Professional benefit maximization software can target the year and month that it is most beneficial for you to file based on your life expectancy.

The three most common ages that people associate with retirement benefits are 62 (Earliest Eligible Age), 66 (Full Retirement Age), and 70 (age at which monthly maximum benefit is reached). In almost all circumstances, however, none of those three most common ages will give you the maximum lifetime benefit.

Remember, every month you wait to file, the amount of your benefit check goes up, but you also get one less check. You don't know how exactly how long you're going to live, but you have a better idea of your life expectancy than the actuaries at the Social Security Administration who can only work with averages. They can't make calculations based on your specific situation. A professional can run the numbers for you and get the target date that maximizes your potential lifetime benefits. You can't get this information from the SSA, but you *can* get it from a financial professional.

Types of Social Security Benefits:

- Retired Worker Benefit. This is the benefit with which most people are familiar. The Retired Worker Benefit is what most people are talking about when they refer to Social Security. It is your benefit based on your earnings and the amount that you have paid into the system over the span of your career.
- Spousal Benefit. This is available to the spouse of someone who is eligible for Retired Worker Benefits.
- Survivorship Benefit. When one spouse passes away, the survivor is able to receive the larger of the two benefit amounts.
- Restricted Application. A higher-earning spouse may be able to start collecting a spousal benefit on the lower-earning spouse's benefit while allowing his or her benefit to continue to grow. Due to the Bipartisan Budget Act of 2015, this option is only available to individuals who turn age 62 before January 1, 2016.

In November of 2015, the Bipartisan Budget Act of 2015 was passed, which will have a dramatic impact on the way many Americans plan for Social Security. As the largest change to Social Security since 2000, the Bipartisan Budget Act of 2015 eliminated an estimated $9.5 billion* of benefits to retirees and may limit some of the flexibility you previously had to structure your benefits.

---

* *https://www.ssa.gov/OACT/progdata/nra.html*

In 2000, Congress passed the Senior Citizens' Freedom to Work Act. The bill allowed retirees to suspend receiving benefits so they wouldn't be subject to additional taxation if they chose to return to work after they filed for Social Security. However, by doing so, the bill also unintentionally created several loopholes in claiming strategies: most notably, the Restricted Application for spousal benefits and "file and suspend" filing strategy. For most Americans, the Bipartisan Budget Act of 2015 closed the loopholes by eliminating "file and suspend" and the Restricted Application.

The new rules mandate that:

- If a primary worker is not currently receiving benefits, then their dependents (child, spouse) can no longer collect benefits based on the primary worker's earning record.
- If you file for benefits, then you are filing for all benefits to which you are entitled – not just the benefit type you choose.

It's important to remember that in spite of these immense changes, one thing stayed the same – filing for Social Security is one of the most important financial decisions you will make in your lifetime, and a financial professional can help ensure you make the right one.

THE DIVORCE FACTOR

How does a divorced spouse qualify for benefits? If you have gone through a divorce, it might affect the retirement benefit to which you are entitled.

In general, a person can receive benefits as a divorced spouse on a former spouse's Social Security record so long as the following conditions are met:

- the marriage lasted at least 10 years; and

- the person filing for divorced benefits is at least age 62, unmarried, and not entitled to a higher Social Security benefit on his or her own record.*

With all of the different options, strategies and benefits to choose from, you can see why filing for Social Security is more complicated than just mailing in the paperwork. Gathering the data and making yourself aware of all your different options isn't enough to know exactly what to do, however. On the one hand, you can knock yourself out trying to figure out which options are best for you and wondering if you made the best decision. On the other hand, you can work with a financial professional who uses customized software that takes all the variables of your specific situation into account and calculates your best option. You have tens of thousands of different options for filing for your Social Security benefit. If your spouse is a different age than you are, it nearly doubles the amount of options you have. This is far more complicated arithmetic than most people can do on their own. If you want a truly accurate understanding of when and how to file, you need someone who will ask you the right questions about your situation, someone who has access to specialized software that can crunch the numbers. The reality is that you need to work with a professional that can provide you with the sophisticated analysis of your situation that will help you make a truly informed decision.

Important Questions about Your Social Security Benefit:
- How can I maximize my lifetime benefit? By knowing when and how to file for Social Security. This usually means waiting until you have at least reached your Full Retirement Age. A professional has the experience and the

---

* *http://www.ssa.gov/retire2/yourdivspouse.html*

tools to help determine when and how you can maximize your lifetime benefits.

- Who will provide reliable advice for making these decisions? Only a professional has the tools and experience to provide you reliable advice.
- Will the Social Security Administration provide me with the advice? The Social Security Administration cannot provide you with advice or strategies for claiming your benefit. They can give you information about your monthly benefit, but that's it. They also don't have the tools to tell you what your specific best option is. They can accurately answer how the system works, but they can't advise you on what decision to make as to how and when to file for benefits.

The Maximization Report that your financial professional will generate represents an invaluable resource for understanding how and when to file for your Social Security benefit. When you get your customized Social Security Maximization Report, you will not only know all the options available to you – but you will understand the financial implications of each choice. In addition to the analysis, you will also get a report that shows exactly at what age – including which month and year – you should trigger benefits and how you should apply. It also includes a variety of other time-specific recommendations, such as when to apply for Medicare or take Required Minimum Distributions from your qualified plans. A report means there is no need to wonder, or to try to figure out when to take action – the Social Security Maximization Report lays it all out for you in plain English.

CHAPTER 4 CHECKLIST //

- To get the most out of your Social Security benefit, you need to file at the right time.
- An Investment Advisor can help you determine when you should file for Social Security to get your Maximum Lifetime Benefit.

5

WILL SOCIAL SECURITY BE ENOUGH?
FILLING THE INCOME GAP

Do you insure your cars? How about your home?
Then why don't you insure what may be your
largest asset… your retirement savings?

Protecting the source of your retirement income gets to the heart of the fear most retirees have of outliving their money. What happens to that fear when you have a guaranteed source of income that cannot be outlived? The fear goes away.

Retirees have many options when it comes to filing the income gap. To review, your income gap, or shortfall, is the difference between the income you need to maintain your lifestyle and the income you know you have coming in during your retirement. So far, guaranteed sources of retirement income may include pension money or Social Security, dividends from stock holdings, money from the sale of real estate, rental property or other sources of income. Your investments might include IRA accounts, 401(k) holdings and stocks or mutual funds. The question now is how do you utilize those investments and savings so they can provide you with guaranteed income?

If you have a known income gap that you need to fill, you want to know how to fill that income gap with the fewest dollars possible. You basically want to buy that income gap for the least amount of money possible. You don't want it to cost you too much, because you want to get the most out of your other assets, including planning for your future and planning for your legacy.

TAKING A HYBRID APPROACH TO YOUR INCOME NEEDS

You looked at Social Security strategies earlier, discovering you have some control over how and when you file. Those decisions can change the outcome of your benefit in your favor. Once you start drawing that income, it is safer and will provide you with a reliable source of income for the rest of your life. While there are many factors of Social Security that you can control, there are many that you cannot.

For example, you do not have the choice of putting more money into Social Security in order to get more out of it. If you could have the option to contribute more money toward Social Security in order to secure a guaranteed income, it would be a great way to create a Green Money asset that would enhance your retirement. Since that option isn't available, you may seek an investment tool that is similar to Social Security that provides you with a reliable income. It also has the potential to increase the value of your principal investment! This kind of win-win situation exists, and it's called an annuity.

Today, you probably have savings in a variety of assets that you acquired over the years. But you may not have taken time to examine them and assess how they will support your retirement. **It's not about whether the market goes up or down, but when it does.** If it goes down at the wrong time for your five or 10 year retirement horizon, you could be in serious danger of losing some of your retirement income. If outliving your money is of concern to you, an annuity may be a good choice. Not only are annuities an investment tool designed for income creation, they effectively work as an insurance policy because the money you invest in these products is guaranteed not to lose value due to stock market loss and any remaining balance can be passed on to your beneficiaries.

Ask yourself the following questions:
- How concerned are you about finding a secure financial vehicle to protect your savings?
- How concerned are you that there may be a better way to structure your savings?

If you are concerned about the best way to fill your income gap, an income annuity investment tool is likely a good option for you. Income annuities have many similar qualities to Social Security that give them the same look and feel as that reliable benefit check you get every month. Most importantly, an income annuity can be an efficient and profitable way to solve your income gap.

HOW ANNUITIES FIT INTO AN OVERALL INCOME PLAN

Annuities are popular and reliable investment tools that allow you to secure income during retirement. In its simplest form, an annuity is a way to invest your money that allows you to structure it for income. Annuities come in a variety of modes. Finding the right one for you will take a conversation with your financial professional. Be sure you fully understand the features, benefits and costs of any annuity you are considering before investing money. The following example shows just how helpful an indexed annuity option can be for a retiree:

> » *Mark and Alicia are 62 years old and have decided to run the numbers to see what their retirement is going to look like. They know they currently need $6,000 per month to pay their bills and maintain their current lifestyle. They have also done their Social Security homework and have determined that, between the two of them, they will receive $4,200 per month in benefits. They also receive $350 per month in rent from a tenant who lives in a small carriage house in their backyard. Between their Social Security and the monthly rent income, they will be short $1,450 per month.*
>
> *They do have an additional asset, however. They have been contributing for years to an IRA that has reached a value of $350,000. They realize that they have to figure out how to turn the $350,000 in their IRA into $1,450 per month for the rest of their life. At first glance, it may seem like they will have plenty of money. With some quick calculations, they find they have 240 months, or nearly 20 years, of monthly income before they exhaust the account. When you consider income tax, the potential for higher taxes in the future, and market fluctuations (because many IRAs are invested in the market), the amount in the IRA seems to have a little less clout. Every dollar Mark and Alicia take out of the IRA is subject to income tax, and if they leave the remainder in the IRA, they run the risk of losing money in a volatile market. Once they retire and stop getting a paycheck every two weeks, they also stop contributing to their IRA. And when they aren't supplementing its growth with their own money, they are*

entirely dependent on market growth. That's a scary prospect. They could also withdraw the money from the IRA and put it in a savings account or CD, but removing all the money at once will put them in a tax bracket that will claim a huge portion of the value of the IRA. A seemingly straightforward asset has now become a complicated equation. Mark and Alicia didn't know what to do, so they met with their financial professional.

Their financial professional suggested that they use the money to purchase an indexed annuity with an income rider. They selected an annuity that was designed for their specific situation. They took the lump sum from their IRA, placed it in an indexed annuity taking advantage of annual reset so they never lost the value of their investment. In return, they were guaranteed the $1,450 of income per month that they needed to meet their retirement goals. The simplicity of the contract allowed them to do an analysis with their professional just once to understand the product. They basically put their money in an investment crockpot where they didn't have to look at it or manage it. They just needed to let it simmer. In fact, their professional was able to find an annuity for them that allowed them their $1,450 monthly payment with a lump sum of $249,455, leaving them more than $100,000 to reinvest somewhere else. Keep in mind that annuities are tax deferred, meaning you will pay tax on the income you receive from an annuity in the year you receive it.

HOW INCOME ANNUITIES WORK

When you put your money into an annuity, you are essentially buying an investment product from an insurance company. It is a contract between you and the insurance company that provides the investment tool. Let's say you have saved $100,000 and need it to generate income to meet your needs above and beyond your

Social Security and pension checks. You give the $100,000 to an insurance company, who in turn invests it to generate growth. They usually select investments that have modest returns over long term horizons. In other words, they generally put it somewhere stable and predictable. Most commonly, they will invest it in a combination of bonds and treasuries that are safer and dependable ways to grow money. They use the money from the insurance products they sell to invest, use a portion of the returns to generate profits for themselves, and return a portion to clients in the form of payouts, claims, and structured income options.

One of the most attractive qualities of these types of annuities is something called annual reset. Annual reset is sometimes also referred to as a "ratcheting." Instead of taking on the risk that comes with putting money in a fluctuating market, you can offset that risk onto the insurance company. It works like this: If the market goes down, you don't suffer a loss. Instead, the insurance company absorbs it. But if the market goes up, you share with the insurance company some of the profit made on the gain. The amount of gain you get is called your annuity participation rate. Typically the insurer will cap the amount of gain you can realize at somewhere between 3 and 7 percent. If the market goes up 10 percent, you would realize a portion of that gain (whatever percentage you are capped at). *It's also worth noting that there are life insurance companies today that offer some very attractive uncapped products that allow investors a much higher potential for gain while still enjoying protection of principal.* This means you to never lose money on your investment, while always gaining a portion of the upswings. The measurement period of your annuity can be calculated monthly, weekly and even daily, but most annuities are measured annually. The level of the index when you buy and the index level one year later will determine the amount of loss or gain. You and the insurance company are betting that the market will generally go up over time.

WHAT IS AN INCOME RIDER?

When you use that $100,000 to buy a contract with an insurance company in the form of an annuity, you are pegging your money on an index. It could be the S&P 500, the Dow Jones Industrial Average or any number of indexes. To generate income from the annuity, you select something called an income rider. An income rider is a subset of an indexed annuity. Essentially, it is the amount of money from which the insurance company will pay you an income while you have your money in their annuity. Your income rider is a larger number than what your investment is actually worth, and if you select the income rider, it will increase in value over time, providing you with more income. As the insurance company holds your money and invests it, they generate a return on it that they use to pay you a regular monthly income based on a higher number. The insurance company has to outperform the amount that they pay you in order to make a profit.

Remember, insurance companies make long-term investments that provide them with predictable flows of money. They like to stabilize the amount of money that goes in and out of their doors instead of paying and receiving large unpredictable chunks at once. When you opt for an income rider, an insurance company can reliably predict how much money they will pay out to you over a set period of time. It's predictable, and they like that. They can base their business on those predictable numbers.

In order to encourage investors to leave their money in their annuity contracts, insurance companies create surrender periods that protect their investments. If you remove your money from the annuity contract during the surrender period, you will pay a penalty and will not be able to receive your entire investment amount back. A typical surrender period is 10 years. If after three years you decide that you want your $100,000 back, the insurance company has that money tied up in bonds and other investments with the understanding that they will have it for another seven

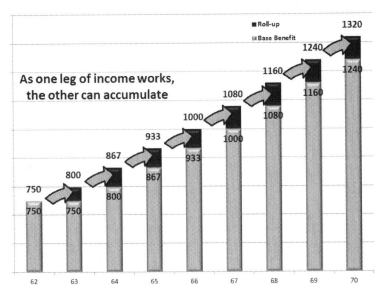

This is a hypothetical illustration

years. Because they will take a hit on removing the money from their investments prematurely, you will have to pay a surrender charge that makes up for their loss. During the surrender period, an annuity is not a demand deposit account like a savings or checking account. The higher returns that you are guaranteed from an annuity are dependent on the timeframe you selected. The longer an insurance company can hold your money, the easier it is for them to guarantee a predictable return on it.

If you leave your money in the annuity contract, you get a reliable monthly income no matter what happens in the market. Once the surrender period has expired, you can remove your money whenever you want. Your money becomes liquid again because the insurance company has used it in an investment that fit the timeline of your surrender period. In addition, most annuities allow for a 10 percent free withdrawal each year essentially making it possible to spend the entire account balance over ten years. For many people, this is an attractive trade off that can provide a creative solution for filling their income gap.

When is an annuity with an income rider right for you? A good financial professional can help you make that determination by taking the time to listen closely to your situation and understanding what your needs are as you enter retirement. Every salesperson has a bag full of brochures and PowerPoint presentations, but they need to know exactly what the financial concerns of their individual clients are in order to help them make the most informed and beneficial decision. Some people need income today, others need it in five or 10 years. Others may have their income needs met but are planning to move closer to their children and will need to buy a house in 10 years. Or, if you want income in 15 years, you might want to choose a different investment product for 10 years, and then switch to an annuity with an income rider during the last five years of your timeline. Everyone's situation is different and everyone's needs are different. People who are interested in annuities, however, usually need to make decisions that affect their income needs, whether it is filling their income gap, or providing for income down the road.

What happens if you place on a shorter timeframe those assets from which you need to draw an income? Something called single premium immediate annuities may be for you:

SINGLE PREMIUM IMMEDIATE ANNUITIES (SPIA)

A single premium immediate annuity is simply a contract between you and an insurance company. SPIAs are structured so that you pay a lump sum of money (a single premium) to an insurance company, and they give you a guaranteed income over an agreed upon time period. That time period could be five years, or it could be for the remainder of your lifetime. Guarantees from insurance companies are based on the claims-paying ability of the issuing insurance company.

SPIAs provide investors with a stream of reliable income when they can't afford to take the risk of losing money in a fluctuating market. While there is general faith that the market always trends up, at least in the long-term, if you are focusing on income over a shorter period of time, you may not be able to take a big hit in the market. Beyond normal market volatility, interest rates also come with an inherent level of uncertainty, making it hard to create a dependable income on your own. SPIAs reduce risk for you by giving you regular monthly, quarterly or yearly payments that can begin the moment you buy the contract. Your financial professional can walk you through a series of different payment options to help you select the one that most closely fits your needs.

Additional Annuity Information:
- Some contracts will allow you to draw income from the high water mark that the market reaches each year. The income rider will then begin calculating its value from the high water mark.
- Income annuities are investment tools that look and feel a bit like Social Security. Every year you allow the money to grow with the market, and it will "roll up" by a specific amount, paying out a specific percent to you as income each year.
- Annuities can work very well to create income, and a financial professional can help you find the one that best matches your income need, and can also structure it to work perfectly for you.

WHAT IS A VARIABLE ANNUITY?
MANAGING RISK WITHIN YOUR ANNUITY

Variable annuities are one kind of annuity that can lose money due to market fluctuations. As their name suggests, they vary with the stock market and the value of the principal (the Account Value) is not guaranteed. If you discover that you have a variable annuity as part of your portfolio, you may want to have it reviewed because these annuities are known for having high fees. Because they are connected to multiple mutual funds, there is usually a fee attached to the management of each fund in addition to Mortality and Expense fees (listed as M&E fees) and administrative fees. The cost of these fees are often not easy to identify on your account statements, so many investors fail to consider the true cost of a variable annuity investment.

If your variable annuity has an income rider on it (and you may not even be aware of this,) the Income Account Value will stay the same or grow, but the value of your *actual* contract may fall. If you surrender the annuity, the insurance company will pay you the market value of the asset, regardless of whether it matches, exceeds or falls short of the value at which you bought the contract. If its value has dropped significantly, you may be better off taking the income rider as an income-for-life stream without surrendering your contract.

Just like any investment strategy, the amount of risk needs to fit the comfort level of the investor. Annuities are no exception. Without going into too much detail, here are some additional ways to manage risk with annuity options:

- Remember that variable annuities can lose money with market fluctuations. These annuities do not take advantage of annual reset when the market goes down. The income rider will stay the same, but the value of your actual contract may fall.

- If you want to structure an annuity investment for growth over a long period of time, be aware that the variable annuity option does not have principal guarantee protection. With a variable annuity, the value of your principal investment follows the market and can lose or gain value with the market. This type of annuity can also have an income rider, but it is really more useful as an accumulation tool that bets on an improving market. A 40-year-old couple, for example, will probably want to structure more for growth and take on more risk than someone in their 70s. The 40-year-old couple may select a variable annuity with an income rider that kicks in when they plan to retire. If it rises with the market or outperforms it, the value of their investment has grown. If the market loses ground over the duration of the contract or their annuity underperforms, they can still rely on the income rider.

- If you are 68 years old and you have more immediate income needs that you need to come up with above and beyond your Social Security, you need a low risk, reliable source of income. If you choose an annuity option, you are looking for something that will pay out an income right away over a relatively short timeframe. You might want to opt for a SPIA that pays you immediately and spans a five year period, as well as an additional income annuity that begins paying you in five years, and another longer term annuity that begins paying you in 10 years.

- Bear in mind that each annuity contract has its own costs and fees. Review these with your financial professional before you determine the best products and strategies for your situation.

» *Jeanne wants to retire at age 68. However, after her Social Security benefit, she will need nearly $375,000 in assets to generate a modest $40,000 of income per year.*

Amazingly, most people don't look ahead to think that at 68 years old, they will need $375,000 to have a basic lifestyle that pays out around $40,000 in addition to their Social Security benefits.

CREATING AN INCOME PLAN

Creating an income plan before you retire allows you to satisfy your need for lifetime income and ensures that your lifestyle can last as long as you do. You also want to create a plan that operates in the most efficient way possible. Doing so will give more security to your retirement nest egg and will potentially allow you to build your legacy down the road.

Here is a basic roadmap of what we have covered so far:

- Review your income needs and look specifically at the shortfall you may have during each year of your retirement based on your Social Security income, and income from any other assets you have.
- Ask yourself where you are in your distribution phase. Is retirement one year away? 10 years away? Last year?
- Determine how much money you need and how you need to structure your existing assets to provide for that need.
- If you have an asset from which you need to generate income, consider options offered by purchasing an income rider on an annuity.

CHAPTER 5 CHECKLIST //

- Do you have a retirement strategy that balances your expected spending with your projected income by funding your projected income gap or shortfall?
- Do you know how and when to take distributions from the various components of your retirement nest egg? Have you consolidated your investments and considered guaranteed products designed to generate income, such as an income annuity? Although an annuity is an income-producing asset, it has the opportunity for growth without subjecting your income to market risk.
- Do you know the amount you can safely withdraw from your nest egg each year so you won't run out of money? Do you understand how to maintain the purchasing power of your money over the course of a lengthy retirement?
- Have you restructured your portfolio to reflect more conservative, Green Money investments that can be used for guaranteed income sources?
- Are you aware of how changes in the economy will affect your pension, investments and retirement income?
- Have you reviewed your portfolio to make sure your investments reflect your income goals and feelings about risk?

6

THE HOPE AND A PRAYER PORTFOLIO

"If you have more than $50,000 to invest, you should fire your broker, and find an investment advisor."

— Arthur Levitt
25th Chairman of the Securities and Exchange Commission

When the market is performing well and investments are making money, every one forgets what happens when the market does badly. During times of recession and market downturn when the news on the T.V. is doom and gloom, you lose sleep at night and then call up your broker to complain. Your broker tells you to wait, ride it out, the market always comes back. Meanwhile your account value drops by 20 percent, then 30 percent, then 40 percent. You assume this is what all retirees do: they spend the bad years hoping and praying their portfolio will somehow pull through. How many more negative years can your retirement portfolio withstand before it runs out of money? Not only is this no way to spend what should be your golden years, it is completely unnecessary.

Once you've gotten a portion of your portfolio in something safe and guaranteed for income generation, we have the ability to use any remaining funds to focus on investments with a long term time horizon. When choosing market investments, many investors make the mistake of going it alone, or worse, they leave the majority of their retirement savings in stock market investments and then start making regular withdrawals to support their income. What typically happens is hoping and praying leads to so much anxiety, the investor panics, takes the money out of the market, and finds that not only have they endured irrevocable loss, but they have also missed out on the opportunity to recover those gains.

HOW TO CRITICIZE YOUR BROKER

As we discussed earlier in Chapter One, many investors don't realize that the financial professional they are working with might not have their best interests in mind. Most stock brokers are required to sell the products and investments offered through their brokerage firm or bank. These firms have a business model they follow in order to meet their sales and profit expectations. While this is business as usual on Wall Street, you don't want the security of your retirement to be at the mercy of inappropriate investment choices and advice. With a bit of knowledge and education, you can learn how to criticize your broker by asking the right questions about the investments you own or are considering owning.

Does this investment have too much risk for your age? Use the Rule of 100 as a rule of thumb to help determine if a Red Money investment is appropriate. Keep in mind that stock brokers DO NOT offer Yellow, Orange or Green Money investments. It's all Red Money.

What is the individual security risk for the stocks or bonds in question? Individual securities risk happens when an investor owns a bucket of individual securities or stock—such as stock for the company they worked for—as opposed to a mix of investments such as those found in a managed Yellow or Orange Money portfolio. The risk of individual securities can be best understood by the following example: imagine you have the majority of your retirement savings invested in General Electric stock. GE is a large company, but during the market downturn of 2008 and 2009, its stock was devalued by as much as 84 percent. What happens to the security of your retirement income?

What is the risk of investing in LOAD or NO LOAD Mutual Funds using a "Buy and Hold" strategy? The *buy and hold* strategy is a prime example of outdated advice that may have worked for our parents but doesn't work for us. The term "load" refers to a commission or fee paid to the broker. Even if you are buying a no load fund, it's the buying and holding of the fund that is the issue. You are essentially riding a roller coaster, hoping and praying that when the ride stops, you'll have enough money to retire on. The problem is, no one can predict the timing of market volatility. Professionally managed portfolios (Yellow and Orange Money) are able to move money and go into a "Risk Off" mode. Instead of buying and holding, they are opportunistic in good times and defensive during bad times. This allows them to protect your money. As mentioned in Chapter Two, you want to look for money managers that are vetted for having a ten year track record or more, with experience in both good markets and bad.

What are the principal trades and mark-up trading profits of the brokerage firm? When you go to a broker to buy an individual stock or bond, they have an inventory or investments to choose from. If a broker dealer has a stock they want to unload, they will mark it up with profit plus a commission and recommend it to other brokers as a great stock. This is a great deal profit wise for the broker, but not a great deal for the client. Furthermore, brokers aren't required to disclose principal mark-up trading. The same thing is also done with bonds.

One way to understand how this works is to take an inside look at how the restaurant industry manages perishable food items such as fish. When the fish is fresh, it is sold for the regular price. A day or two before it starts to go bad, the chef will recognize the fish is about to turn, and he or she will concoct a sauce and run a special. The server who can sell the most fish receives some kind of prize. The chef is able to unload a larger quantity of the fish, the server gets a prize, but what does the diner get? The possibility of a stomach ache and a meal that is not as good as it could have been.

An investment advisor held to fiduciary standards gets paid the same regardless of when or how the stock is bought or sold. There are no incentives for unloading toxic products because their fees are locked-in and fully disclosed.

What is the interest rate risk and maturity risk on bonds? Some bonds sold to seniors have an unreasonable amount of interest rate risk or maturity risk to the investor. It's important to note that this risk does not apply to all bonds. Consider Al who is 70 years old. He is sold a 30-year bond by his broker dealer because it pays an attractive rate of return, and an excellent commission to the broker, but Al doesn't realize that he will be 100 years old before that bond matures. If he needs the money, he may have to sell the bond at a loss.

What is "credit and default" risk for buy and hold Corporate Investment Grade Bonds or High Yield Bonds? Bonds can be used as part of an overall growth strategy, but it's important to be aware that not all bonds are rated the same. A low rated bond may have some associated credit risk or default risk if it's a high risk bond. For example, if you buy a corporate investment grade bond issued by Company XYZ, and that company goes bankrupt, what is their bond worth to you?

What is the risk of purchasing a preferred stock? Preferred stocks are more volatile than common stock. You'll know if you own a preferred stock because it will be listed right on your statement. The term "preferred" indicates the investment will generate a higher dividend, because the holder of preferred stock receives their dividend payouts first, before the common stock holder. This sounds like a good deal, but in general these stocks are typically more volatile and may not be the best investment choice for a retiree.

What is the risk of closed-end mutual funds, or Real Estate and Unit Investment Trusts? (REITS and UITs): Many of these investments are non-tradable, which means you may not be able to get out of them when you need to. While most stock market investments are known for being liquid—meaning you can liquidate the investment and access the cash within 30 days—these investments aren't as liquid as they appear. They also pay out high commissions—as high as 15 percent—to the broker dealer.

HOW TO OUTLIVE YOUR MONEY

When you are managing your money by yourself, emotions inevitably enter into the mix. The Dow Jones Industrial Average and the S&P 500 represent more to you than market fluctuations. They represent your retirement dreams. It's hard not to be emotional about it.

Everyone knows you should buy low and sell high. But this is what is more likely to happen:

The market takes a downturn, similar to the 2008 crash, and investors see as much as a 30 percent loss in their stock holdings. It's hard to watch, and it's harder to bear the pain of losing that much money because it takes even larger gains just to get back to where things were before the downturn. They sell. But eventually, and inevitably, the market begins to rise again. Maybe slowly, maybe with some moderate growth, but by the time the average investor notices an upward trend and wants to buy in again, they have already missed a great deal of the gains.

» *Hannah worked for a paper mill company for 34 years. During her time there, she acquired bonuses and pay raises that often included shares of stock in the company. She also dedicated part of her paycheck every month to a 401(k) that bought stock in the company. By the time she retired, Hannah has $250,000 worth of company stock.*

Although she had contributed to her 401(k) account every month, Hannah didn't cultivate any other assets that could generate income for her during retirement. Hannah also retired early at age 62 because of her failing health. The commute to work every day was becoming difficult in her weakened condition and she wanted to enjoy the rest of her life in retirement instead of working in the cramped office of the restaurant supply company.

Because she retired early, Hannah failed to maximize her Social Security benefit. While she lives a modest lifestyle, her income needs are $3,500 per month. Hannah's monthly Social Security check only covers $1,900, leaving her with a $1,600 income gap. To supplement her Social Security check, Hannah sells $1,600 of company stock each month to meet her income needs. A $250,000 401(k) is nothing to sneeze at, but reducing its value by $1,600 every month will decimate her savings within 10 years. And that's if the market stays neutral or grows modestly. If the market takes a downturn, the money that Hannah relies on to fill her income gap will rapidly diminish. Even if the market starts going up in a couple of years, it will take much larger gains for her to *recover the value that she lost due to the math of rebounds (which will be explained shortly).*

Unhappily for Hannah, she retired in 2007, just before the major market downturn that lasted for several years. She lost more than 20 percent of the value of her stock. Because Hannah needed to sell her stock to meet her basic income needs, the market price of the stock was secondary to her need for the money. When she needed money, she was forced to sell however many shares she needed to fill her income gap that month. And if she has a financial crisis, involving a need for long term medical care, for example, she will be forced to sell stock even if the market is low and her shares are nearly worthless.

Hannah realizes that she could have relied on an investment structured to deliver her a regular income while protecting the value of her investment. She could have kept her $250,000 from diminishing while enjoying her lifestyle into retirement regardless of the volatility of the market. Ideally, Hannah would have restructured her 401(k) to reflect the level of risk that she was able to take. In her case, she would have had most of her money in Green Money investments so her hard-earned money could support her when she needed it.

WHAT THE DALBAR STUDY FOUND

In 2013, DALBAR, the well-respected financial services market research firm, released their annual "Quantitative Analysis of Investment Behavior" report (QAIB). The report studied the impact of market volatility on individual investors: people like Hannah, or anyone who was managing (or mismanaging) their own investments in the stock market.

According to the study, volatility not only caused investors to make decisions based on their emotions, those decisions also harmed their investments and prevented them from realizing potential gains. So why do people meddle so much with their investments when the market is fluctuating? Part of the reason is that many people have financial obligations that they don't have control over. Significant expenses like house payments, the unexpected cost of replacing a broken-down car, and medical bills can put people in a position where they need money. If they need to sell investments to come up with that money, they don't have the luxury of selling when they *want* to. They must sell when they *need* to.

DALBAR's "Quantitative Analysis of Investor Behavior" has been used to measure the effects of investors' buying, selling and mutual fund switching decisions since 1994. The QAIB shows time and time again over nearly a 20 year period that the average investor earns less, and in many cases, significantly less than the performance of mutual funds suggests. QAIB's goal is to improve independent investor performance and to help financial professionals provide helpful advice and investment strategies that address the concerns and behaviors of the average investor.

An excerpt from the report claims that:*

"QAIB offers guidance on how and where investor behaviors can be improved. No matter what the state of the mutual fund industry, boom or bust: Investment results are more dependent on investor behavior than on fund performance. Mutual fund investors who hold on to their investments are more successful than those who time the market.

QAIB uses data from the Investment Company Institute (ICI), Standard & Poor's and Barclays Capital Index Products to compare mutual fund investor returns to an appropriate set of benchmarks.

There are actually three primary causes for the chronic shortfall for both equity and fixed income investors:

---

*2013 QAIB, Dalbar, March 2013

1. *Capital not available to invest. This accounts for 25 percent to 35 percent of the shortfall.*
2. *Capital needed for other purposes. This accounts for 35 percent to 45 percent of the shortfall.*
3. *Psychological factors. These account for 45 percent to 55 percent of the shortfall."*

The key findings of Dalbar's QAIB report provide compelling statistics about how individual investment strategies produced negative outcomes for the majority of investors:

- Psychological factors account for 45 percent to 55 percent of the chronic investment return shortfall for both equity and fixed income investors.
- Asset allocation is designed to handle the investment decision-making for the investor, which can materially reduce the shortfall due to psychological factors.
- Successful asset allocation investing requires investors to act on two critical imperatives:
    1. Balance capital preservation and appreciation so that they are aligned with the investor's objective.
    2. Select a qualified allocator.
- The best way for an investor to determine their risk tolerance is to utilize a risk tolerance assessment. However, these assessments must be accessible and usable.
- Evaluating allocator quality requires analysis of the allocator's underlying investments, decision making process and whether or not past efforts have produced successful outcomes.
- Choosing a top allocator makes a significant difference in the investment results one will achieve.
- Mutual fund retention rates suggest that the average investor has not remained invested for long enough periods to derive the potential benefits of the investment markets.

- Retention rates for asset allocation funds exceed those of equity and fixed income funds by over a year.
- Investors' ability to correctly time the market is highly dependent on the direction of the market. Investors generally guess right more often in up markets. However, in 2012 investors guessed right only 42 percent of the time during a bull market.
- Analysis of investor fund flows compared to market performance further supports the argument that investors are unsuccessful at timing the market. Market upswings rarely coincide with mutual fund inflows while market downturns do not coincide with mutual fund outflows.
- Average equity mutual fund investors gained 15.56 percent compared to a gain of 15.98 percent that just holding the S&P 500 produced.
- The shortfall in the long-term annualized return of the average mutual fund equity investor and the S&P 500 continued to decrease in 2012.
- The fixed-income investor experienced a return of 4.68 percent compared to an advance of 4.21 percent on the Barclays Aggregate Bond Index.
- The average fixed income investor has failed to keep up with inflation in nine out of the last 14 years.*

It doesn't take a financial services market research report to tell you that market volatility is out of your control. The report does prove, however, that before you experience market volatility, you should have an investment plan, and when the market is fluctuating, you should stand by your investment plan. You should also review and discuss your investment plan with your financial professional on a regular basis, ensuring he/she is aware of any changes in your

*2013 QAIB, Dalbar, March 2013

goals, financial circumstances, your health or your risk tolerance. When the economy is under stress and the markets are volatile, investors can feel vulnerable. That vulnerability causes people to tinker with their portfolios in an attempt to outsmart the market. Financial professionals, however, don't try to time the market for their clients. They try to tap into the gains that can be realized by committing to long-term investment strategies.

CHAPTER 6 CHECKLIST //

- Have you calculated how many more -20, - 30, or -40 percent investment return years your investment portfolio can take? It's easy to forget about the bad times during the stock market good times.
- Do you know how to criticize your broker? Have you asked him or her about the risks inherent in the investments they sell to you such as credit and default risk, preferred stock risk and the risk of closed end mutual funds, to name a few?
- Do you understand how emotions affect the decision making skills of the average investor playing the stock market alone? According to the DALBAR "Quantitative Analysis of Investment Behavior" report released in 2013, the average fixed income investor managing his or her money alone failed to keep up with inflation in nine out of the last 14 years.
- Do you understand the difference between a Red Money investment and a Yellow or Orange Money portfolio designed for the individual as part of an overall income plan?

7

WHAT IS YELLOW AND ORANGE MONEY?

As you read earlier in the key findings of the DALBAR report, the deck is stacked against the individual investor. Remember that the average fixed income investor failed to keep pace with inflation in nine of the last 14 years, meaning the inherent risk in managing your Red Money is very real and could have a lasting impact on your assets. So, how much of your Red Money do you invest, and in what kinds of markets, investment products and stocks?

There are a lot of different directions in which you can take your Red Money. One thing is for sure: significant accumulation depends on investing in the market. How you go about doing it is different for everyone. Gathering stocks, bonds and investment funds together in a portfolio without a cohesive strategy behind them could cause you to miss out on the benefits of a more thoughtful and planful approach. The end result is that you may never really understand what your money is doing, where and how it is really invested, and which investment principles are behind the investment products you hold. While you may have goals for each individual piece of your portfolio, it is likely that you don't have a comprehensive plan for your Red Money, which may mean that *you are taking on more risk than you would like, and are getting less return for it than is possible.*

Enter ***Yellow OR Orange Money.*** As introduced earlier in Chapter Two, Yellow Money is Red Money that is being managed in a conservative growth portfolio; Orange Money is Red Money that is being managed in a moderate growth portfolio. In both cases, the money is managed by a professional *with a purpose.* After your income needs are met and you have assets that you would like to dedicate to accumulation, there are decisions you need to make about how to invest those assets. You can buy stocks, index funds, mutual funds, bonds — you name it — you can invest in it. However, the difference between Red Money and Yellow or Orange Money is that Yellow and Orange Money has a cohesive strategy behind it that is *implemented by a professional.* When you manage your Red Money with an investment plan, it changes color because the risk is mitigated. *Money that is being managed with a specific purpose, a specific set of focused goals and a specific strategy in mind has considerably less risk and volatility than Red Money, yet still provides excellent returns over time.* Yellow or Orange Money is still a type of Red Money that comes with different levels of risk. But Yellow and Orange Money is under the watchful eye of professionals who have a stake in the success of your money in the market and who can recommend a range of strategies from those designed for preservation to those targeting rapid growth. You don't want to miss out on achieving the right level of risk, and more importantly, composing a careful plan for the return of your assets.

Investment advisors held to the fiduciary oath have a vested interest in their clients. They only grow if you grow. Their success is linked to your success. How does it feel to know that your broker's income can be going up even while your account value is going down?

Another way to look at the difference between Red Money and Yellow or Orange Money is with this analogy:

If you needed to travel through an unfamiliar city in a foreign country, you could rent a car or perhaps hire a driver. Were you to drive yourself, you would try to gain guidance from perplexing road signs and need to adhere to traffic rules—with no experience or assistance to lean on. It would take longer to get to where you want to go, and the chance of a traffic accident would be higher. If you hired a driver, they would manage your journey. A driver would know the route, how to avoid traffic, and follow the rules of the road.

Red Money is like driving yourself. With Yellow and Orange Money, you are still traveling by car, but now you have a professional working on your behalf. Yellow and Orange Money are not considered Green Money, but these investment have considerably less risk and volatility than Red Money, while potentially outperforming the returns that Red Money promises.

TAKING A CLOSER LOOK AT YOUR PORTFOLIO

Think about your investment portfolio. Think specifically of what you would consider your Red Money. Do you know what is there? You may have several different investment products like individual mutual funds, bond accounts, stocks, etc. You may have inherited a stock portfolio from a relative, or you might be invested in a bond account offered by the company for which you worked due to your familiarity with them. While you may or may not be managing your investments individually, the reality is that you probably don't have an overall management strategy for all of your investments. Investments that aren't managed are simply Red Money, or money that is at risk in the market.

Harnessing the earning potential of your Red Money relies on more than a collection of stocks and bonds, however. It needs guided management. A good portfolio manager uses the knowledge they have about the level of risk with which you are comfortable, what you need or want to use your money for, when you want or need it and how you want to use it. The Yellow or Orange Money investments that they choose for you will still have a certain level of risk, but under the right management, control and process, you have a far better chance of a successful outcome that meets your specific needs.

When you sit down with an investment professional, you can look at all of your assets together. Chances are that you have accumulated a number of different assets over the last 20, 30 or 50 years. You may have a 401(k), an IRA, a Roth IRA, an account of self-directed stocks, a brokerage account, etc. Wherever you put your money, a financial professional will go through your assets and help you determine the level of risk to which you are exposed now and should be exposed in the future.

Here is a typical example of how an investment professional can be helpful to a future retiree with Yellow Money needs:

» *Kristin is 65 years old and wants to retire in two years. She has a 401(k) from her job to which she has contributed for 26 years. She also has some stocks that her late husband managed. Kristin also has $55,000 in a mutual fund that her sister recommended to her five years ago and $30,000 in another mutual fund that she heard about at work. She takes a look at her assets one day and decides that she doesn't understand what they add up to or what kind of retirement they will provide. She decides to meet with an investment professional. Kristin's professional immediately asks her:*

94

1. *Does she know exactly where all of her money is?* *Kristin doesn't know much about all her husband's stocks, which have now become hers. Their value is at $100,000 invested in three large cap companies. Kristin is unsure of the companies and whether she should hold or sell them.*
2. *Does she know what types of assets she owns?* *Yes and no. She knows she had a 401(k) and IRAs, but she is unfamiliar with her husband's self-directed stock portfolio or the type of mutual funds she owns. Furthermore she is unclear as to how to manage the holdings as she nears retirement.*
3. *Does she know the strategies behind each one of the investment products she owns?* *While Kristin knows she had a 401(k), an IRA and mutual fund holdings, she doesn't know how her 401(k) is organized or how to make it more conservative as she nears retirement. She is unsure whether her IRA is a Roth or traditional variety and how to draw income from them? She really does not have specific investment principles guiding her investment decisions, and she doesn't know anything about her husband's individual stocks. One major concern for Kristin is whether her family would be okay if she were not around?*

After determining Kristin's assets, her financial professional prepares a consolidated report that lays out all of her assets for her to review. Her professional explains each one of them to her. Kristin discovers that although she is two years away from retiring, her 401(k) is organized with an amount of risk with which she is not comfortable. Sixty percent of her 401(k) is at risk, far off the mark if we abide by the Rule of 100. Kristin opts to be more conservative than the Rule of 100 suggests, as she will rely on her 401(k) for most of her immediate income needs after retirement. Kristin's professional also points out several instances of overlap between her mutual funds. Kristin learns that while she is comfortable with one of her mutual funds, she does not agree with the management principles of the other. In the end, Kristin's professional helps her re-organize her 401(k) to secure her more Green Money for retirement income. Her professional also uses her mutual fund and her husband's stock assets to create a growth oriented investment plan that Kristin will rely on for Need Later Money in 15 years when she plans on relocating closer to her children and grandchildren. By creating an overall investment strategy, Kristin is able to meet her targeted goals in retirement. Kristin's financial professional worked closely with her and her tax professional to minimize the tax impact of any asset sales on Kristin's situation.

Like Kristin, you may have several savings vehicles: a 401(k), an IRA to which you regularly contribute, some mutual funds to which you make monthly contributions, etc. But what is your *overall investment strategy?* Do you have one in place? Do you want one that will help you meet your retirement goals? Yellow or Orange Money portfolios look at *ALL* your accounts and all their different strategies to create a plan that helps them all work together.

AVOIDING EMOTIONAL INVESTING

There's no way around it; people get emotional about their money. And for good reason. You've spent your life working for it, exchanging your time and talent for it, and making decisions about how to invest it, save it and make it grow. The maintenance of your lifestyle and your plans for retirement all depend on it. The best investment strategies, however, don't rely on emotions. One of Yellow and Orange Money's greatest strengths lies in the fact that it is managed by someone who understands your needs and desires, but doesn't make decisions about your money under the influence of emotion.

A well-managed investment account meets your goals as a whole, not in individualized and piecemeal ways. Professional money managers do this by creating requirements for each type of investment in which they put your money. We'll call them "screens." Your money manager will run your holdings through the screens they have created to evaluate different types of investment strategies. A professionally managed account will only have holdings that meet the requirements laid out in the overall management plan that was designed to meet your investment goals. The holdings that don't make it through the screens, the ones that don't contribute to your investment goals, are sold and redistributed to investments that your financial professional has determined to be appropriate.

Different screens apply to different Yellow and Orange Money strategies. For example, if one of your goals is significant growth, which would require taking on more risk alongside the potential for more return, an investment professional would screen for companies that have high rates of revenue and sales growth, high earnings growth, rising profit margins, and innovative products. On the other hand, if you want your portfolio to be used for income, which would call for lower risk and less return, your professional would screen for dividend yield and sector diversification. *Every investor has a different goal, and every goal requires a customized strategy that uses quantitative screens.* A professional will create a portfolio that reflects your investment desires. If some of the current assets you own complement the strategies that your professional recommends, those will likely stay in your portfolio.

Screening your assets removes emotions from the equation. It removes attachment to underperforming or overly risky investments. Financial professionals aren't married to particular stocks or mutual funds for any reason. They go by the numbers and see your portfolio through a lens shaped by your retirement goals. Your professional understands your wants and needs, and creates an investment strategy that takes your life events and future plans into account. It's a planful approach, and it allows you to tap into the tools and resources of a professional who has built a career around successful investing. Managing money is a full-time job and is best left to a professional money manager.

Removing emotions from investing also allows you to be unaffected by the day-to-day volatility of the market. Your financial professional doesn't ask where the market is going to be in a year, three years or a month from now. If you look at the value of the stock market from the beginning of the twentieth century to today, it's going up. Despite the Great Depression, despite the 1987 crash, despite the 2008 market downturn, the market, as a whole, trends up. Remember the major market downturn in 2008 when the market lost 37 percent of its value? Not only did it completely recover, it has far exceeded its 2008 value. Emotional investing led countless people to sell low as the market went down, and buy the same shares back when the market started to recover. That's an expensive way to do business. While you can't afford to lose money that you need in 5, 10, or 20 years, this later income money does have time to grow. The best way to achieve that growth safely is to make it Orange or Yellow.

> » *Ian is 69 years old. He retired four years ago. He relied on income from an IRA for three years in order to increase his Social Security benefit. He also made significant investments in 36 different mutual funds. He chose to diversify among the funds by selecting a portion for growth, another for good dividends, another that focused on promising small cap companies and a final portion that work like index funds. All the money that Ian had in mutual funds he considered money that he wanted to rely on in his 80s. After the stock market took a hit in 2008, Ian lost some confidence in his invest-*

ments and decided to sit down with a financial professional to see if his portfolio was able to recover.

The professional Ian met with was able to determine what goals he had in mind. Specifically, the financial professional determined what Ian actually wanted and needed the money for, and when he needed it. His professional also looked inside each of the mutual funds and discovered several instances of overlap.

While Ian had created diversity in his portfolio by selecting funds focused on different goals, he didn't account for overlap in the companies in which the funds were invested. Out of the 36 funds, his professional found that 20 owned nearly identical stock. While most of the companies were good investments, the high instance of overlap did not contribute to the healthy investment diversity that Ian wanted. Ian's financial professional also provided him with a report that explained the concentration ratio of his holdings (noting how much of his portfolio was contained within the top 25 stock holdings), the percentage of his portfolio that each company in which he invested in represented (showing the percentage of net assets that each company made up as an overall position in his portfolio) and the portfolio date of his account (showing when the funds in his portfolio were last updated: as funds are required to report updates only twice per year, it was possible that some of his fund reports could be six months old).

Ian's professional consolidated his assets into one investment management strategy. This allowed Ian's investments to be managed by someone he trusted who knew his specific investment goals and needs. Eliminating redundancy and overlap in his portfolio was easy to do but difficult to detect since Ian had multiple funds with multiple brokerage firms. Ian sat down with a professional to see if his mutual funds could perform well, and he left with a consolidated man-

agement plan and a money manager that understood him personally. That's managed money at its best.

CREATING AN INVESTMENT STRATEGY

Just like Ian and Kristin, chances are that you can benefit from taking a more managed investment approach tailored to your goals. Yellow or Orange Money is generally money that you want to grow for income needs you'll have in at least 10 years. You can work with your financial planner to create investments that meet your needs within different timeframes. You may need to rely on some of your Yellow or Orange Money in 10, 15 or 20 years, whether for additional income, a large purchase you plan on making or a vacation. Whatever you want it for, you will need it down the road. A financial professional can help you rescale the risk of your assets as they grow, helping you lock in your profits and secure a source of income you can depend on later.

So what does a Yellow or Orange Money account look like? Here's what it *doesn't* look like: a portfolio with 49 small cap mutual funds, a dozen individual stocks and an assortment of bond accounts. A brokerage account with a hodgepodge of investments, even if goal-oriented, is not a professionally managed account. It's still Red Money. Remember, Yellow and Orange Money is a managed account that has an overarching investment philosophy. When you look at making investments that will perform to meet your future income needs, the burning question becomes: How much should you have in the market and how should it be invested? Working with a professional held to fiduciary standards will help you determine how much risk you should take, how to balance your assets so they will meet your goals and how to plan for the big ticket items, like health care expenses, that may be in your future. Yes, Yellow and Orange Money is exposed to risk, but by working with a professional who has your best interests in mind, you can manage that risk in a productive way.

WHY YELLOW OR ORANGE MONEY?

If you have met your immediate income needs for retirement, why bother with professionally managing your other assets? The money you have accumulated above and beyond your income needs probably has a greater purpose. It may be for your children or grandchildren. You may want to give money to a charity or organization that you admire. In short, you may want to craft your legacy. It would be advantageous to grow your assets in the best manner possible. A financial professional has built a career around managing money in profitable ways. They are experts under the supervision of the organization that they represent.

Turning to Yellow or Orange Money also means that you don't have to burden yourself with the time commitment, the stress, and the cost of determining how to manage your money. A managed money portfolio can help you better enjoy your retirement. Do you want to sit down in your home office every day and determine how to best allocate your assets, or do you want to be living your life, enjoying your golden years while someone else manages your money for you? When the majority of your Red Money is managed with a specific purpose by a financial professional, you don't have to be worrying about which stocks to buy and sell today or tomorrow.

SEEKING FINANCIAL ADVICE: STOCK BROKERS VS. INVESTMENT ADVISOR REPRESENTATIVES

As covered early in Chapter Two, investors basically have access to two types of advice in today's financial world: advice from stock brokers and advice given by investment advisors. Most investors don't know the difference between types of advice and the people from whom they receive advice. In a survey taken by

TD Ameritrade, the top reasons investors choose to work with an independent registered investment advisor are:*

- Registered Investment Advisors are required, as fiduciaries, to offer advice that is in the best interest of clients
- More personalized service and competitive fee structure offered at a Registered Investment Advisor firm
- Dissatisfaction with full commission brokers

Confusion continues to exist among investors struggling to find the best and most credible financial advice out there. Here is some additional information to help clear up the confusion so you can find good advice from a professional you can trust:

- Investment advisor representatives have the fiduciary duty to act in a client's best interest at all times with every investment decision they make.
- Stock brokers and brokerage firms usually do not act as fiduciaries to their investors and are not obligated to make decisions that are entirely in the best interest of their customers. For example, if you decide you want to invest in precious metals, a stock broker would offer you a precious metals account from their firm. An Investment Advisor would find you a precious metals account that is the best fit for you based on the investment strategy of your portfolio.
- Investment advisors give their clients a Form ADV describing the methods that the professional uses to do business. An Investment Advisor also obtains client consent regarding any conflicts of interest that could exist with the business of the professional.

2011 Advisor Sentiment Study, commissioned by TD AMERITRADE. TD Ameritrade, Inc.

- Stock brokers and brokerage firms are not obligated to provide comparable types of disclosure to their customers.
- Whereas stock brokers and firms routinely earn large profits by trading as principal with customers, Investment Advisors cannot trade with clients as principal (except in very limited and specific circumstances).
- Investment Advisors charge a pre-negotiated fee with their clients in advance of any transactions. They cannot earn additional profits or commissions from their customers' investments without prior consent. Registered Investment Advisors are commonly paid an asset-based fee that aligns their interests with those of their clients. Brokerage firms and stock brokers, on the other hand, have much different payment agreements. Their revenues may increase regardless of the performance of their customers' assets.
- Unlike brokerage firms, where investment banking and underwriting are commonplace, Registered Investment Advisors must manage money in the best interests of their customers. Because Registered Investment Advisors charge set fees for their services, their focus is on their client. Brokerage firms may focus on other aspects of the firm that do not contribute to the improvement of their clients' assets.
- Unlike brokers, Registered Investment Advisors do not get commissions from fund or insurance companies for selling their investment products.

Just to drive home the point, here is what a fiduciary duty to a client means for a Registered Investment Advisor. Registered Investment Advisors must:*

- Always act in the best interest of their client and make investment decisions that reflect their goals.
- Identify and monitor securities that are illiquid.
- When appropriate, employ fair market valuation procedures.
- Observe procedures regarding the allocation of investment opportunities, including new issues and the aggregation of orders.
- Have policies regarding affiliated broker-dealers and maintenance of brokerage accounts.
- Disclose all conflicts of interest.
- Have policies on use of brokerage commissions for research.
- Have policies regarding directed brokerage, including step-out trades and payment for order flow.
- Abide by a code of ethics.

*2011 Advisor Sentiment Study, commissioned by TD AMERITRADE. TD Ameritrade, Inc.

CHAPTER 7 CHECKLIST //

- Do you understand the difference between a Yellow or Orange Money portfolio as compared to the high-risks of Red Money investments?
- Do you have a strategy in place to grow the money you don't need for income now? Does this strategy have a dedicated direction, strategy and end goal in mind to mitigate the risk of more growth-focused investments?
- Do you understand why professionals manage growth portfolios without emotions? A financial professional qualified to manage growth portfolios uses specific criteria designed to fit into your overall financial plan so that it works the way you want it to.
- Does your financial professional have your best interest in mind? Are they held to fiduciary or suitability standards of liability?

8

NEW PERSPECTIVES FOR INVESTING

"The difficulty lies not in the new ideas,
but in escaping from the old ones."
– John Maynard Keynes

Throughout this book, we have discussed how today, investment options requires advice that is relevant to today. Traditional, outdated investment strategies are not only ineffective; they can be harmful to the average investor. One of the most traditional ways of thinking about investing is the risk versus reward trade-off. It goes something like this:

Investment options that are considered safer carry less risk, but also offer the potential for less return. Riskier investment options carry the burden of volatility and a greater potential for loss, but they also offer a greater potential for large rewards. Most professionals move their clients back and forth along this range, shifting between investments that are safer and investments that are structured for growth. Essentially, the old rules of investing dictate that you can either choose relative safety *or* return, but you can't have both.

EVERY INVESTMENT HAS A LIQUIDITY COST

Updating your investment strategy to utilize new products and portfolio management strategies allows you to capitalize on greater returns and greater safety. Using the three bucket approach, you can achieve a balance of safety and return, using strategies that work with the flexibility of liquidity to remake the rules. Here is how:

There are three dimensions that are inherent in any investment: *Liquidity, Safety, and Return*. You can maximize any two of these dimensions at the expense of the third. If you choose Safety and Liquidity, this is like keeping your assets in a checking account or savings account. This option delivers a lot of Safety and Liquidity, but at the expense of any Return. On the other hand, if you choose Liquidity and Return, meaning you have the potential for great return and can still reclaim your money whenever you choose, you will likely be exposed to a very high level of risk.

Using the three bucket approach, you can balance your portfolio to capitalize on the strengths of all three, *liquidity, safety, and return.*

Bucket A: The funds in your Green Money bucket are strongest in the area of *safety* with an appealing rate of *return*. These investments are safe and secure—you cannot lose your principal and you cannot lose your gains with the money in your Green Bucket. These investments generally speaking offer more limited liquidity, but for all practical purposes, you can spend all the money in your green money bucket in 10 years. Do you have a plan in place that has you spending all your money in 10 years?

Bucket B: The funds in your Yellow Money bucket offer stronger growth than your Green Money bucket and lower risk and lower volatility than Red Money. Yellow Money investments can usually offer 100 percent liquidity with conservative growth and the safety that comes from a managed investment strategy.

Bucket C: The funds in your Orange Money bucket are strongest in the area *return*. They offer about the same liquidity options as your Yellow Money bucket but because the risk is moderate, Orange Money can be said to have less safety than Green Money.

Understanding Liquidity can help you break the old Risk versus Safety trade-off. By identifying assets from which you don't require Liquidity, you can place yourself in a position to potentially profit from relatively safe investments that provide a higher than average rate of return.

Choosing Safety and Return over Liquidity can have significant impacts on the accumulation of your assets. In the following example of Andy and his liquid investment portfolio, the paradigm shift from earning and saving to leveraging assets is a costly one:

» *Andy is a corn and soybean farmer with 1,200 acres of land. He routinely retains somewhere between $40,000 and $80,000 in his checking and savings accounts. If a major piece of equipment fails and needs repair or replacement, Andy will need the money available to pay for the equipment and carry on with farming. If the price of feed for his cattle goes up one year, he will need to compensate for the increased overhead to his farming operation. He isn't a particularly wealthy farmer, but he has little choice but to keep a portion* *of money on hand in case something comes up and he must access it quickly. Most of his capital is held in livestock in the pasture or crops in the ground tied up for six to eight months of the year. When a major financial need arises, Andy can't just harvest 10 acres of soybeans and use them for payment. He needs to depend heavily on Liquidity in order to be a successful farmer.*

Old habits die hard, however, and when Andy finally hangs up his overalls and quits farming, he keeps his bank accounts flush with cash, just like in the old days. After selling the farm and the equipment, Andy keeps a huge portion of the profits in Liquid investments because that's what he is familiar with. Unfortunately for Andy, with his pile of money sitting in his checking account, he isn't even keeping pace with inflation. After all his hard work as a farmer, his money is losing value every day because he didn't shift to a paradigm of leveraging his assets to generate income and accumulate value.

Almost anything would be a better option for Andy than clinging to Liquidity. He could have done something better to get either more return from his money or more safety, and at the very least would not have lost out to inflation.

YOUR LAZY MONEY

The establishment of an emergency fund is key to achieving a successful balance of safety, liquidity and return. Ideally, this fund consists of $20,000 to $40,000 or roughly six months of living expenses. This is what you can think of as your lazy money: it's lying around in a bathrobe and slippers, not doing much of anything. Its only job is to be there when you need it, and as such, safety and liquidity are its chief objectives. Your lazy money is best left lounging around in a money market or savings account where it can be easily accessed in the case of an emergency or unexpected expense such as car repairs.

Taking out a large sum of money from a qualified account can trigger a tax event; pulling the money from your income producing assets could cause a monetary shortfall down the road. Having the money in a safe, easy-to-access lazy account means you can sleep at night knowing that no matter what financial emergency life may bring, you have the funds covered.

How much do you need to have in your emergency fund? The amount of an emergency fund will vary greatly depending on the individual situation of the retiree. Four to six months of income is a commonly used amount, but there can be legitimate reasons why that amount could be more or less.

The question is, how much Liquidity do you *really* need? Think about it. If you haven't sat down and created an income plan for your retirement, your perceived need for Liquidity is a guess. You don't know how much cash you'll need to fill the income gap if you don't know the amount of your Social Security benefit of the total of your other income options. If you *have* determined your income need and have made a plan for filling your income gap, you can partition your assets based on when you will need them. With an income plan in place, ***you'll have a new perspective on how to enjoy both Safety and Return from your assets.***

CHAPTER 8 CHECKLIST //

- Do you understand the trade-off between liquidity, safety, and return that is inherent in any investment? You can choose to maximize any two against the third.
- Do you understand the liquidity costs of your investments? Maximizing liquidity alone can be an expensive option because the sooner you need your money back, the less you can leverage it for safety and return.
- Have you identified your needs for liquidity by establishing a lazy money emergency fund? Ideally you want to have up to 6 months of living expenses set aside in a liquid account that can be easily accessed.

9
TAXES AND RETIREMENT

*You will make more money saving on taxes than
you will by making more money.*

Everyone is familiar with taxes (you've been paying them your entire working life), but not everyone is familiar with how to make tax planning a part of their retirement strategy.

Tax planning and *tax reporting* are two very different things. Most people only *report* their taxes. March rolls around, people pull out their 1040s or use TurboTax to enter their income and taxable assets, and ship it off to Uncle Sam at the IRS. If you use a CPA to report your taxes, you are essentially paying them to record history. You have the option of being proactive with your taxes and to plan for your future by making smart, informed decisions about how taxes affect your overall financial plan. Working with a financial professional who, along with a CPA, makes recommendations about your finances to you, will keep you looking forward instead of in the rearview mirror as you enter retirement.

HOW TO PAY LESS TAX DURING YOUR RETIREMENT

When you retire, you move from the earning and accumulation phase of your life into the asset distribution phase of your life. For most people, that means relying on Social Security, a 401(k), an IRA, or a pension. Wherever you have put your *Know So* Money for retirement, you are going to start relying on it to provide you with the income that once came as a paycheck. Most of these distributions will be considered income by the IRS and will be taxed as such. There are exceptions to that (not all of your Social Security income is taxed, and income from Roth IRAs is not taxed), but for the most part, your distributions will be subject to income taxes.

Regarding assets that you have in an IRA, when you reach 70½ years of age, you will be required to draw a certain amount of money from your IRA as income each year. That amount depends on your age and the balance in your IRA. The amount that you are required to withdraw as income is called a Required Minimum Distribution (RMD). Why are you required to withdraw money from your own account? Chances are the money in that account has grown over time, and the government wants to collect taxes on that growth. If you have a large balance in an IRA, there's a chance your RMD could increase your income significantly enough to put you into a higher tax bracket, subjecting you to a higher tax rate.

Here's where tax planning can really begin to work strongly in your favor. In the distribution phase of your life, you have a predictable income based on your RMDs, your Social Security benefit and any other income-generating assets you may have. What really impacts you at this stage is how much of that money you keep in your pocket after taxes. Essentially, ***you will make*** *more money saving on taxes than you will by making more money.* If you can reduce your tax burden by 30, 20 or even 10 percent, you earn yourself that much more money by not paying it in taxes.

How do you save money on taxes? By having a plan. In this instance, a financial professional can work with the CPAs at their firm to create a **distribution plan** that minimizes your taxes and maximizes your annual net income.

BUILDING A TAX DIVERSIFIED PORTFOLIO

So far so good: avoid taxes, maximize your net annual income and have a plan for doing it. When people decide to leverage the experience and resources of a financial professional, they may not be thinking of how distribution planning and tax planning will benefit their portfolios. Often more exciting prospects like planning income annuities, investing in the market and structuring investments for growth rule the day. Taxes, however, play a crucial role in retirement planning. Achieving those tax goals requires knowledge of options, foresight and professional guidance.

Finding the path to a good tax plan isn't always a simple task. Every tax return you file is different from the one before it because things constantly change. Your expenses change. Planned or unplanned purchases occur. Health care costs, medical bills, an inheritance, property purchases, reaching an age where your RMD kicks in or travel, any number of things can affect how much income you report and how many deductions you take each year.

Preparing for the ever-changing landscape of your financial life requires a tax-diversified portfolio that can be leveraged to balance the incomes, expenditures and deductions that affect you each year. A financial professional will work with you to answer questions like these:

- What does your tax landscape look like?

- Do you have a tax-diversified portfolio robust enough to adapt to your needs?
- Do you have a diversity of taxable and non-taxable income planned for your retirement?
- Will you be able to maximize your distributions to take advantage of your deductions when you retire?
- Is your portfolio strong enough and tax-diversified enough to adapt to an ever-changing (and usually increasing) tax code?

» *When Penny returns home after a week in the hospital recovering from a knee replacement, the 77-year-old calls her daughter, sister and brother to let them know she is home and feeling well. She also should have called her CPA. Penny's medical expenses for the procedure, her hospital stay, her medications and the ongoing physical therapy she attended amount to more than $50,000.*

Currently, Americans can deduct medical expenses that are more than 7.5 percent of their Adjusted Gross Income (AGI). Penny's AGI is $60,000 the year of her knee replacement, meaning she is able to deduct $44,000 of her medical bills from her taxes that year. Her AGI dictated that she could deduct more than 80 percent of her medical expenses that year. **Penny didn't know this.**

Had she been working with a financial professional who regularly asked her about any changes in her life, her spending, or her expenses (expected or unexpected), Penny could have saved thousands of dollars. Penny can also file an amendment to her tax return to recoup the overpayment.

This relatively simple example of how tax planning can save you money is just the tip of the iceberg. No one can be expected to know the entire U.S. tax code. But a professional who is working with a team of CPAs and financial professionals have an advantage over the average taxpayer who must start from square one on their own every year. Have you been taking advantage of all the deductions that are available to you?

PROACTIVE TAX PLANNING

The implications of proactive tax planning are far reaching, and are larger than many people realize. Remember, doing your taxes in January, February, March or April means you are writing a history book. Planning your taxes in October, November or December means that you are writing the story as it happens. You can look at all the factors that are at play and make decisions that will impact your tax return *before* you file it.

Realizing that tax planning is an aspect of financial planning is an important leap to make. When you incorporate tax planning into your financial planning strategy, it becomes part of the way you maximize your financial potential. Paying less in taxes means you keep more of your money. Simply put, the more money you keep, the more of it you can leverage as an asset. This kind of planning can affect you at any stage of your life. If you are 40 years old, are you contributing the maximum amount to your 401(k) plan? Are you contributing to a Roth IRA? Are you finding ways to structure the savings you are dedicating to your children's education? Do you have life insurance? Taxes and tax planning affects all of these investment tools. Having a relationship with a professional who works with a CPA can help you build a truly comprehensive financial plan that not only works with your investments, but also shapes your assets to find the most efficient ways to prepare for tax time. There may be years that you could benefit from higher distributions because of the tax bracket that you are in, or there could be years you would benefit from taking less. There may be years when you have a lot of deductions and years you have relatively few. **Adapting your distributions to**

work in concert with your available deductions is at the heart of smart tax planning. Professional guidance can bring you to the next level of income distribution, allowing you to remain flexible enough to maximize your tax efficiency. And remember, saving money on taxes makes you more money than making money does. What you have on paper is important: your assets, savings, investments, which are financial expression of your work and time. It's just as important to know how to get it off the paper in a way that keeps most of it in your pocket. Almost anything that involves financial planning also involves taxes. Annuities, investments, IRAs, 401(k)s, 403(b), and many other investment options will have tax implications. Life also has a way of throwing curveballs. Illness, expensive car repair or replacement, or *any event that has a financial impact on your life will likely have a corresponding tax implication* around which you should adapt your financial plan. Tax planning does just that. **One dollar can end up being less than 25 cents to your heirs.**

» *When Jerry's father passed away, he discovered that he was the beneficiary of his father's $500,000 IRA. Jerry has a wife and a family of four children, and he knew that his father had intended for a large portion of the IRA to go toward funding their college educations.*

After Jerry's father's estate is distributed, Jerry, who is 50 years old and whose two oldest sons are entering college, liquidates the IRA. By doing so, his taxable income for that year puts him in a 39.6 percent tax bracket, immediately reducing the value of the asset to $302,000. An additional 3.8 percent surtax on net investment income further diminishes the funds to $283,000. Liquidating the IRA in effect subjects much of Jerry's regular income to the surtax, as well. At this point, Jerry will be taxed at 43.4 percent.

Jerry's state taxes are an additional 9 percent. Moreover, estate taxes on Jerry's father's assets claim another 22 percent. By the time the IRS is through, Jerry's income from the IRA will be taxed at 75 percent, leaving him with $125,000 of the original $500,000. While it would help contribute to the education of his children, it wouldn't come anywhere near completely paying for it, something the $500,000 could have easily done.

As the above example makes clear, leaving an asset to your beneficiaries can be more complicated than it may seem. In the case of a traditional IRA, after federal, estate and state taxes, the asset could literally diminish to as little as 25 percent of its value.

How does working with a professional help you make smarter tax decisions with your own finances? Any financial professional worth their salt will be working with a firm that has a team of trained tax professionals, including CPAs, who have an intimate knowledge of the tax code and how to adapt a financial plan to it.

Here's another example of how taxes have major implications on asset management:

> *» Henry and Alice, a 62-year-old couple, begin working with a financial professional in October. After structuring their assets to reflect their risk tolerance and creating assets that would provide them income during retirement, they feel good about their situation. They make decisions that allow them to maximize their Social Security benefits, they have plenty of options for filling their income gap, and they have a strategy in place for emergency funds and growth opportunities. When their professional asks them about their tax plan, they tell him their CPA handled their taxes every year, and did a great job. Their professional says, "I don't mean who does your taxes, I*

mean, who does your tax planning?" Henry and Alice aren't sure how to respond.

Their professional brings Henry and Alice's financial plan to the firm's CPA and has her run a tax projection for them. A week later their professional calls them with a tax plan for the year that will save them more than $3,000 on their tax return. The couple is shocked. A simple piece of advice from the CPA based on the numbers revealed that if they paid their estimated taxes before the end of the year, they would be able to itemize it as a deduction, allowing them to save thousands of dollars.

This solution won't work for everyone, and it may not work for Henry and Alice every year. That's not the point. By being proactive with their approach to taxes and using the resources made available by their financial professional, they were able to create a tax plan that saved them money.

MANAGED MONEY AND TAXES

There are also tax implications for the money that you have managed professionally. People with portions of their investment portfolio that are actively traded can particularly benefit from having a proactive tax strategy. Without going into too much detail, for tax purposes there are two kinds of investment money: qualified and non-qualified. Different investment strategies can have different effects on how you are taxed on your investments and the growth of your investments. Some are more beneficial for one kind of investment strategy over another. Determining how to plan for the taxation of non-qualified and qualified investments is fodder for holiday party discussions at accounting firms. While it may not be a stimulating topic for the average investor, you don't have to understand exactly how it works in order to benefit from it.

While there are many differences between qualified and non-qualified investments, the main difference is this: qualified plans are designed to give investors tax benefits by deferring taxation of their growth until they are withdrawn. Non-qualified investments are not eligible for these deferral benefits. As such, non-qualified investments are taxed whenever income is realized from them in the form of growth.

Actively and non-actively traded investments provide a simple example of how to position your investments for the best tax advantage. In an actively traded and managed portfolio, there is a high amount of buying and selling of stocks, bonds, funds, ETFs, etc. If that active portfolio of non-qualified investments does well and makes a 20 percent return one year and you are in the 39.6 percent tax bracket, your net gain from that portfolio is only about 12 percent (39.6 percent tax of the 20 percent gain is roughly 8 percent.) In a passive trading strategy, you can use a qualified investment tool, such as an IRA, to achieve 13, 14 or 15 percent growth (much lower than the actively traded portfolio), but still realize a higher net return because the growth of the qualified investment is not taxed until it is withdrawn.

Does this mean that you have to always rely on a buy and hold strategy in qualified investment tools? Not necessarily. The question is, if you have qualified and non-qualified investments, where do you want to position your actively traded and managed assets? Incorporating a planful approach to positioning your investments for more beneficial taxation can be done many ways, but let's consider one example. Keeping your actively managed investment strategies inside an IRA or some other qualified plan could allow you to realize the higher gains of those investments without paying tax on their growth every year. Your more passively managed funds could then be kept in taxable, non-qualified vehicles and methods, and because you aren't realizing income from them on an annual basis by frequently trading them, they grow sheltered from taxation.

If you are interested in taking advantage of tax strategies that maximize your net income, you need the attentive strategies, experience and knowledge of a professional who can give you options that position you for profit. At the end of the day, what's important to you as the consumer is how much you keep, your after-tax take home.

ESTATE TAXES

The government doesn't just tax your income from investments while you're alive. They will also dip into your legacy.

While estate taxes aren't as hot of a topic as they were a few years ago, they are still an issue of concern for many people with assets. While taxes may not apply on estates that are less than $5 million, certain states have estate taxes with much lower exclusion ratios. Some are as low as $600,000. Many people may have to pay a state estate tax. One strategy for avoiding those types of taxes is to move assets outside of your estate. That can include gifting them to family or friends, or putting them into an irrevocable trust. Life insurance is another option for protecting your legacy.

CHAPTER 9 CHECKLIST //

- Are you planning for your taxes during retirement, or merely reporting them? When you *plan* your taxes with a financial professional, you are proactively finding the best options for your tax return. Knowing how to use tax law in your favor means putting more money in your wallet.

- Are you educated about tax-wise withdrawal strategies and aware that it's more advantageous to withdraw assets from taxable accounts before tapping into those that are tax-deferred?

- Have you considered the tax repercussions before tapping into assets from a 401(k) or a traditional IRA for use as an income source? Money that is considered qualified by the Federal government must be taxed upon distribution.

- Do you know your RMD birthday? At the age of 70 ½, the Federal Government requires all IRA participants to take their RMD, or Required Minimum Distribution. Failure to take your RMD can cost you thousands of dollars in taxes and penalty fees.

10
THE FUTURE OF U.S. TAXATION

Qualified retirement plan account balances are very deceiving because the money is not all yours to keep. You have a silent partner during your distribution years who will take 25 to 40 percent of your income. His name is Uncle Sam.

Tax legislation over the course of American history has left one very resounding message: taxes go up. Sadly, we hear this same threat so often that it has begun to sound like the boy who cried wolf. The reason behind this lies in the fact that tax hikes usually do not take effect until two or three years after their introduction and subsequently get piecemeal implementation. The result of this prolonged implementation period can be equated to death by a thousand paper cuts.

DEBT CEILING – CAUSE AND EFFECTS

The raising of the debt ceiling raised more than just the ability for our government to go further into debt. It also raised concerns and fears about the future of our economy. We are now seeing major swings in the markets with investors showing serious concerns over the future of investment valuations and their personal wealth. Unfortunately, the reasoning behind all of this uncertainty is preceded by the inability to see the full implications of what is in store. We rarely talk about the fact that the discussions on raising the debt ceiling were coupled to discussions on major tax reforms needed to correct the problems underlining the debt ceiling increase itself.

Increasing the debt ceiling was needed because the government maxed out its credit card, so to speak, which it has been living off of for quite some time. It is really not much different than what we have been seeing from the general public for the past few decades. Unfortunately, most of us do not have the ability to get a credit limit increase on our credit cards once we reach the maximum limit, that is unless we can show the ability to pay this balance back. The only way to pay this credit card back is by spending less and making more money.

This is exactly where the federal government is today. They have been given a higher credit limit, but they still must find a way to decrease the spending while making more money. The only way the government makes money is by collecting taxes.

Unfortunately, at the current moment, the government is collecting approximately $120 billion less per month than it currently spends. Discussions for major tax reform have accompanied the discussions for the increased debt ceiling.

DEBT AND EARNINGS

Let us take a closer look at where we are today. The U.S. national debt is increasing at an alarming rate, rising to levels never seen before and threatening serious harm to the economy. Through the end of 2010, the national debt has risen to $13.6 trillion, averaging an 11.4 percent increase annually over the past five years and a 9.2 percent increase annually over the past 10 years. To put this into perspective, the national gross domestic product (GDP) has increased to $14.5 trillion during the same period, averaging a 2.9 percent annual increase over the past five years and a 3.9 percent increase over the past 10 years. At the end of 2010, the national debt level was 93 percent of the GDP. Economists believe that a sustainable economy exists at a maximum level of approximately 80 percent. As of December 20, 2013, the U.S. national debt is 107.69 percent of GDP with the debt at $17.252 trillion and the GDP at $16.020 trillion.*

The significance of these two numbers lies within the contrast. The national debt is the amount that needs to be repaid. This is the credit card balance. Gross domestic product on the other hand is less known and represents the market value of all final goods and services produced within a country during a given period. Essentially, GDP represents the gross taxable income available to the government. If debts are increasing at a greater rate than the gross income available for taxation, then the only way to make up the difference is by increasing the rate at which the gross income is taxed.

The most recent presidential budget shows a continuing trend in the disparity between growth in the national debt and GDP over the next two decades. Although the increasing disparity is a real concern and shows that, at least in the short run, the federal deficit will not be addressed to counteract the potential crisis ahead, it is the revenue collection that tells the disconcerting story. Over the past 40 years the average collection of GDP has

---

http://www.usdebtclock.org/12/20/13

been approximately 17.6 percent and currently collections are at approximately 14.4 percent of GDP.

As the presidential budget reveals, the projected revenues are estimated to be 20 percent by the end of the next decade. That is a 38.8 percent increase from the current tax levels. To put this into perspective, if you are currently in the top tax bracket of 35 percent and this bracket increases by the proposed collection increase, your tax rate will be approximately 48.5 percent. Keep in mind that even at this rate the deficit is projected to increase.

2013 – THE END OF AN ERA?

From a historical point of view, taxes are extremely low. The last time the U.S. national debt was at the same percentage level of GDP as today was at the end of World War II and several years following. The maximum tax rate averaged 90 percent from 1944 through 1963. Compare that to the maximum rate of 35 percent today and it becomes very clear that there is a disparity of extreme proportion.

Taxes during this historical period were at extreme levels for nearly 20 years, during and following this current level of debt-to-GDP. A significant point to note about the difference between that time and today is the economic activity. The period of 1944 through 1963 was in the heart of both the industrial revolution and the birth of the Baby Boom generation. Today, we are mired in extreme volatility with frequent periods of boom and bust at the same time we are witnessing the beginning of the greatest retirement wave ever experienced within the U.S. economy.

To contrast these two time periods in respect to the recovery period is almost asinine as the external pressures from globalization and domestic unfunded liabilities did not exist or were irrelevant factors during the prior period.

To add insult to injury, U.S. domestic unfunded liabilities are currently estimated somewhere around $61.6 trillion due to items such as Social Security, Medicare and government pensions. The most concerning part of this pertains to the coming wave of retirement as the Baby Boom generation begins retiring and drawing on the unfunded Social Security for which they currently have entitlement. Over the long run, expenditures related to healthcare programs such as Medicare and Medicaid are projected to grow faster than the economy overall as the population matures.

To put unfunded liabilities into perspective, consider these as off-balance-sheet obligations similar to those of Enron. Although these are not listed as part of the national debt, they must be paid. These liabilities exist outside of the annual budgetary debt discussed. The difference between Enron and the U.S. unfunded liabilities is that if the U.S. government cannot come up with the funds to pay all these liabilities through revenue generation, they will print the money necessary to pay the debt.

WHAT DOES THE SOLUTION LOOK LIKE?

Unfortunately, the general public is in a no-win situation for this solution to the problem. Printing money does not bode well for economic growth. This creates inflationary pressures that devalue the U.S. dollar and make everyone less wealthy. Cutting the entitlements that compose this liability leaves millions of people with lower benefits than they have come to expect. The only other option, and one that the government knows all too well, is increasing taxes. In fact, according to a Congressional Budget Office paper issued in 2004:

"The term 'unfunded liability' has been used to refer to a gap between the government's projected financial commitment under a particular program and the revenues that are expected to be available to fund that commitment. But no government obligation can be truly considered 'unfunded' because of the U.S. government's sovereign power to tax—which is the ultimate resource to meet its obligations."

A balanced budget will be required at some point and with this will come higher taxes. We have uncertainty surrounding tax rates and how high they will go. At that time, extensions put in place in December 2010 on Bush-era tax cuts are set to expire. We are likely to see some tax increases at this point. Whether it is only on the top earners or unilaterally across all income levels is yet to be seen, but an increase of some sort will most certainly occur.

How do you prepare? Why spend so much time reassuring you that taxes will increase? Because you have an opportunity to take action. Now is the time to prepare for what will come and structure countermeasures for the good, the bad and the ugly of each of these legislative nightmares through tax-advantaged retirement planning.

You make more money by saving on taxes than you do by making more money. The simplistic logic of the statement makes sense when you discover it takes $1.50 in earnings to put that same dollar, saved in taxes, back in your pocket.

As simple as it sounds, it is much more difficult to execute. Most people fail to put together a plan as they near retirement, beginning with a simple cash flow budget. If you have not analyzed your proposed income streams and expenses, you could not possibly have taken the time to position these cash flows and other events into a tax-preferred plan.

Most people will state that they have a plan and, thus, do not need any further assistance in this area. The truth in most instances is that people could not show you their plan, and among the few that could, most would not be able to show you how they have executed it. In this regard, they might as well be Richard Nixon stating, "I am not a crook" for as much as they state, "I have a plan." The truth lies in waiting. As we approach or begin retirement, we should look at what cash flows we will have. Do we have a pension? How about Social Security? How much additional cash flow am I going to need to draw from my assets to maintain the lifestyle that I desire?

We spend our whole lives saving and accumulating wealth but spend so little time determining how to distribute this accumulation so as to retain it. We need to make sure we have the appropriate diversification of taxable versus non-taxable assets to complement our distribution strategy.

THE BENEFITS OF DIVERSIFICATION

Heading into retirement, we should be situated with a diversified tax landscape. The point to spending our whole lives accumulating wealth is not to see the size of the number on paper, but rather to be an exercise in how much we put in our pocket after removing it from the paper. To truly understand tax diversification, we must understand what types of money exist and how each of these will be treated during accumulation and, most importantly, during distribution. The following is a brief summary:

1. Free money
2. Tax-advantaged money
3. Tax-deferred money
4. Taxable money
   a. Ordinary income
   b. Capital gains and qualified dividends

FREE MONEY

Free money is the best kind of money regardless of tax treatment because, in the end, you have more money than you would have otherwise. Many employers will provide contributions toward employee retirement accounts to offer additional employment benefits and encourage employees to save for their own retirement. With this, employers often will offer a matching contribution in which they contribute up to a certain percentage of an employee's salary (generally three to five percent) toward that employee's retirement account when the employee contributes to their retirement account as well. For example, if an employee earns $50,000 annually and contributes three percent ($1,500) to their retirement account annually, the employer will also contribute three percent ($1,500) to the employee's account. That is $1,500 in free money. Take all you can get! Bear in mind that any employer contribution to a 401(k) will still be subject to taxation when withdrawn.

TAX-ADVANTAGED MONEY

Tax-advantaged money is the next best thing to free money. Although you have to earn tax-advantaged money, you do not have to give part of it away to Uncle Sam. Tax-advantaged money comes in three basic forms that you can utilize during your lifetime; four if prison inspires your future, but we are not going to discuss that option.

One of the most commonly known forms of tax-advantaged money is municipal bonds, which earn and pay interest that could be tax-advantaged on the federal level, or state level, or both. There are several caveats that should be discussed with regard to the notion of tax-advantaged income from municipal bonds. First, you will notice that tax-advantaged has several flavors from the state and federal perspective. This is because states will generally tax the interest earned on a municipal bond unless the bond is offered from an entity located within that state. This severely limits the availability of completely tax-advantaged municipal bonds and constrains underlying risk and liquidity factors. Second, municipal bond interest is added back into the equation for determining your modified adjusted gross income (MAGI) for Social Security. This could push your income above a threshold and subject a portion of your Social Security income to taxation.

In effect, if this interest subjects some other income to taxation then this interest is truly being taxed.

Last, municipal bond interest may be excluded from the regular federal tax system, but it is included for determining tax under the alternative minimum tax (AMT) system. In its basic form, the AMT system is a separate tax system that applies if the tax computed under AMT exceeds the tax computed under the regular tax system. The difference between these two computations is the alternative minimum tax.

TAX-ADVANTAGED MONEY: ROTH IRA

Roth accounts are probably the single greatest tax asset that has come from Congress. They are well known but rarely used. Roth IRAs were first established by the Taxpayer Relief Act of 1997 and named after Senator William Roth, the chief sponsor of the legislation. Roth accounts are simply an account in the form of an individual retirement account or an employer sponsored retirement account that allows for tax-advantaged growth of earnings and, thus, tax-advantaged income.

The main difference between a Roth and a traditional IRA or employer-sponsored plan lies in the timing of the taxation. We are all very familiar with the typical scenario of putting money away for retirement through an employer plan, whereby they deduct money from our paychecks and put it directly into a retirement account. This money is taken out before taxes are calculated, meaning we do not pay tax on those earnings today. A Roth account, on the other hand, takes the money after the taxes have been removed and puts it into the retirement account, so we do pay tax on the money today. The other significant difference between these two is taxation during distribution in later years. Regarding our traditional retirement accounts, when we take the money out later it is added to our ordinary income and is taxed accordingly. Additionally, including this in our income subjects us to the consequences mentioned above for municipal bonds with Social Security taxation, AMT, as well as higher Medicare premiums. A Roth on the other hand is distributed tax-advantaged and does not contribute toward negative impact items such as Social Security taxation, AMT, or Medicare premium increases. It essentially comes back to us without tax and other obligations. The best way to view the difference between the two accounts is to look at the life of a farmer. A farmer will buy seed, plant it in the ground, grow the crops and harvest it later for sale. Typically, the farmer would only pay tax on the crops that have been harvested and sold. But if you were the farmer, would you rather pay tax on the $5,000 of seed that you plant today or the $50,000 of crops harvested later? The obvious answer is $5,000 of seed today. The truth to the matter is that you are a farmer, except you plant dollars into your retirement account instead of seeds into the earth.

So why doesn't everyone have a Roth retirement account if things are so simple? There are several reasons, but the single greatest reason has been the constraints on contributions. If you earned over certain thresholds (MAGI over $125,000 single and $183,000 joint for 2012), you were not eligible to make contributions, and until last year, if your modified adjusted gross income (MAGI) was over $100,000 (single or joint), you could not convert a traditional IRA to a Roth. Outside these contribution limits, most people save for retirement through their employers and most employers do not offer Roth options in their plans. The reason behind this is because Roth accounts are not that well understood and people have been educated to believe that saving on taxes today is the best possible course of action.

TAX-DEFERRED MONEY

Tax-deferred money is the type of money with which most of people are familiar, but we also briefly reviewed the idea above. Tax-deferred money is typically our traditional IRA, employer sponsored retirement plan or a non-qualified annuity. Essentially, you put money into an investment vehicle that will accumulate in value over time and you do not pay taxes on the earnings that grow these accounts until you distribute them. Once the money is distributed, taxes must be paid. However, the same negative consequences exist with regard to additional taxation and expense in other areas as previously discussed. The cash accumulation value can be used for tax-advantaged income.

TAXABLE MONEY

Taxable money is everything else and is taxable today, later or whenever it is received. These four types of money come down to two distinct classifications: taxable and tax-free. The greatest difference when comparing taxable and tax-advantaged income is a function of how much money we keep after tax. For help in determining what the differences should be, excluding outside factors such as Social Security taxation and AMT, a tax equivalent yield should be used.

TAX-ADVANTAGED IN THE REAL WORLD

To put the tax equivalent yield into perspective, let us look at an example: Rick and Mary are currently retired, living on Social Security and interest from investments and fall within the 25 percent tax bracket. They have a substantial portion of their investments in municipal bonds yielding 6 percent, which is quite comforting in today's market. The tax equivalent yield they would need to earn from a taxable investment would be 8 percent, a 2 percent gap that seems almost impossible given current market volatility. However, something that has never been put into perspective is that the interest from their municipal bonds is subject to taxation on their Social Security benefits (at 21.25 percent). With this, the yield on their municipal bonds would be 4.725 percent, and the taxable equivalent yield falls to 6.3 percent, leaving a gap of only 1.575 percent.

In the end, most people spend their lives accumulating wealth through the best, if not the only vehicle they know, a tax-deferred account. This account is most likely a 401(k) or 403(b) plan offered through our employer and may be supplemented with an IRA that was established at one point or another. As the years go by, people blindly throw money into these accounts in an effort to save for a retirement that we someday hope to reach.

The truth is, most people have an age selected for when they would like to retire, but spend their lives wondering if they will ever be able to actually quit working. To answer this question, you must understand how much money you will have available to contribute toward your needs. *In other words, you need to know what your after-tax income will be during this period.*

All else being equal, it would not matter if you put your money into a taxable, tax-deferred or tax-advantaged account as long as income tax rates never change and outside factors are never an event. The net amount you receive in the end will be the same.

Unfortunately, this will never be the case. We already know that taxes will increase in the future, meaning we will likely see higher taxes in retirement than during our peak earning years.

Regardless, saving for retirement in any form is a good thing as it appears from all practical perspectives that future government benefits will be cut and taxes will increase. You have the ability to plan today for efficient tax diversification and maximization of our after-tax dollars during your distribution years.

CHAPTER 10 CHECKLIST //

- Are you prepared for the future of U.S. taxation? Do you understand the benefits of tax diversification?
- Are you familiar with tax-deferred methods of retirement savings such a traditional IRAs? By taking action now, you can prepare for an increase in taxes by restructuring your assets to include the benefits of free and tax-advantaged money.
- Do you have tax-advantaged income you can rely on for income during your retirement? One of the most common forms of tax-advantaged money includes municipal bonds, but be aware these come with many state and federal caveats and complexities.
- Are you taking advantage of Roth IRAs and life insurance as two forms of tax-advantaged money? These tools can help you take advantage of today's lower tax rate when preparing for tomorrow's retirement.

11

THE BRANDEIS STORY

Louis Brandeis provides one of the best examples illustrating how tax planning works. Brandeis was Associate Justice on the Supreme Court of the United States from 1916 to 1939. Born in Louisville, Kentucky, Brandeis was an intelligent man with a touch of country charm. He described tax planning this way:

"I live in Alexandria, Virginia. Near the Court Chambers, there is a toll bridge across the Potomac. When in a rush, I pay the dollar toll and get home early. However, I usually drive outside the downtown section of the city and cross the Potomac on a free bridge.

The bridge was placed outside the downtown Washington, D.C. area to serve a useful social service—getting drivers to drive the extra mile and help alleviate congestion during the rush hour.

If I went over the toll bridge and through the barrier without paying a toll, I would be committing tax evasion.

*If I drive the extra mile and drive outside the city of Washington to the free bridge, I am using a legitimate, logical and suitable method of tax avoidance, and I am performing a useful social service by doing so. The tragedy is that **few people know that the free bridge exists.**"*

Like Brandeis, most American taxpayers have options when it comes to "crossing the Potomac," so to speak. It's a financial planner's job to tell you what options are available. You can wait until March to file your taxes, at which time you might pay someone to report and pay the government a larger portion of your income. However, you could instead file before the end of the year, work with your financial professional and incorporate a tax plan as part of your overall financial planning strategy. Filing later is like crossing the toll bridge. Tax planning is like crossing the free bridge. Which would you rather do?

The answer to this question is easy. Most people want to save money and pay less in taxes. What makes this situation really difficult in real life, however, is that the signs along the side of the road that direct us to the free bridge are not that clear. To normal Americans, and to plenty of people who have studied it, the U.S. tax code is easy to get lost in. There are all kinds of rules, exceptions to rules, caveats and conditions that are difficult to understand, or even to know about. What you really need to know is your options and the bottom line impacts of those options.

ROTH IRA CONVERSIONS

The attractive qualities of Roth IRAs may have prompted you to explore the possibility of moving some of your assets into a Roth account. Another important difference between the accounts is how they treat Required Minimum Distributions (RMDs). When you turn 70 ½ years old, you are required to take a minimum amount of money out of a traditional IRA. This amount is your

RMD. It is treated as taxable income. Roth IRAs, however, do not have RMDs, and their distributions are not taxable. Quite a deal, right?

While having a Roth IRA as part of your portfolio is a good idea, converting assets to a Roth IRA can pose some challenges, depending on what kinds of assets you want to transfer. One common option is the conversion of a traditional IRA to a Roth IRA. You may have heard about converting your IRA to a Roth IRA, but you might not know the full net result on your income. The main difference between the two accounts is that the growth of investments within a traditional IRA is not taxed until income is withdrawn from the account, whereas taxes are charged on contribution amounts to a Roth IRA, not withdrawals. The problem, however, is that when assets are removed from a traditional IRA, even if the assets are being transferred to a Roth IRA account, taxes apply.

There are a lot of reasons to look at Roth conversions. People have a lot of money in IRAs, up to multiple millions of dollars. Even with $500,000, when they turn 70 ½ years old, their RMD is going to be approximately $18,000, and they have to take that out whether they want to or not. It's a tax issue. Essentially, if you will be subject to high RMDs, it could have impacts on how much of your Social Security is taxable, and on your tax bracket.

By paying taxes now instead of later on assets in a Roth IRA, you can realize tax-advantaged growth. You pay once and you're done paying. Your heirs are done paying. It's a powerful tool. Here's a simple example to show you how powerful it can be:

Imagine that you pay to convert a traditional IRA to a Roth. You have decided that you want to put the money in a vehicle that gives you a tax-advantaged income option down the road. If you pay a 25 percent tax on that conversion and the Roth IRA then doubles in value over the next 10 years, you could look at your situation as only having paid 12.5 percent tax.

The prospect of tax-advantaged income is a tempting one. While you have to pay a conversion tax to transfer your assets, you also have turned taxable income into tax free retirement money that you can let grow as long as you want without being required to withdraw it.

There are options, however, that address this problem. Much like the Brandeis story, there may be a "free bridge" option for many investors.

Your financial professional will likely tell you that it is not a matter of whether or not you should perform a Roth IRA conversion, it is a matter of how much you should convert and when.

Here are some of the things to consider before converting to a Roth IRA:

- If you make a conversion before you retire, you may end up paying higher taxes on the conversion because it is likely that you are in some of your highest earning years, placing you in the highest tax bracket of your life. It is possible that a better strategy would be to wait until after you retire, a time when you may have less taxable income, which would place you in a lower tax bracket.

- Many people opt to reduce their work hours from fulltime to part-time in the years before they retire. If you have pursued this option, your income will likely be lower, in turn lowering your tax rate.

- The first years that you draw Social Security benefits can also be years of lower reported income, making it another good time frame in which to convert to a Roth IRA.

One key strategy to handling a Roth IRA conversion is to *always be able to pay the cost of the tax conversion with outside money*. Structuring your tax year to include something like a significant deduction can help you offset the conversion tax. This way you aren't forced to take the money you need for taxes from the value of the IRA. The reason taxes apply to this maneuver is because when you withdraw money from a traditional IRA, it is treated as taxable income by the IRS. Your financial professional, with the help of the CPAs at their firm, may be able to provide you with options like after-tax money, itemized deductions or other situations that can pose effective tax avoidance options.

Some examples of avoiding Roth IRA conversions taxes include:

- *Using medical expenses that are above 10 percent of your Adjusted Gross Income.* If you have health care costs that you can list as itemized deductions, you can convert an amount of income from a traditional IRA to a Roth IRA that is offset by the deductible amount. Essentially, deductible medical expenses negate the taxes resulting from recording the conversion.

- *Individuals, usually small business owners, who are dealing with a Net Operating Loss (NOL).* If you have NOLs, but aren't able to utilize all of them on your tax return, you can carry them forward to offset the taxable income from the taxes on income you convert to a Roth IRA.

- *Charitable giving.* If you are charitably inclined, you can use the amount of your donations to reduce the amount of taxable income you have during that year. By matching the amount you convert to a Roth IRA to the amount your taxable income was reduced by charitable giving, you can essentially avoid taxation on the conversion. You may decide to double your donations to a charity in one year, giving them two years' worth of donations in order to offset the Roth IRA conversion tax on this year's tax return.

- *Investments that are subject to depletion.* Certain investments can kick off depletion expenses. If you make an investment and are subject to depletion expenses, they can be deducted and used to offset a Roth IRA conversion tax.

Not all of the above scenarios work for everyone, and there are many other options for offsetting conversion taxes. The point is that you have options, and your financial professional and tax professional can help you understand those options.

If you have a traditional IRA, Roth conversions are something you should look at. As you approach retirement you should consider your options and make choices that keep more of your money in your pocket, not the government's.

ADDITIONAL TAX BENEFITS OF ROTH IRAS

Not only do Roth IRAs provide you with tax-advantaged growth, they also give you a tax diversified landscape that allows you to maximize your distributions. Chances are that no matter the circumstances, you will have taxed income and other assets subject to taxation. *But if you have a Roth IRA, you have the unique ability to manage your Adjusted Gross Income (AGI), because you have a tax-advantaged income option!*

Converting to a Roth IRA can also help you preserve and build your legacy. Because Roth IRAs are exempt from RMDs, after you make a conversion from a traditional IRA, your Roth account can grow tax-advantaged for another 15, 20 or 25 years and it can be used as tax-advantaged income by your heirs. It is important to note, however, that non-spousal beneficiaries do have to take RMDs from a Roth IRA, or choose to stretch it and draw tax-advantaged income out of it over their lifetime.

TO CONVERT OR NOT TO CONVERT?

Conversions aren't only for retirees. You can convert at any time. Your choice should be based on your individual circumstances and tax situation. Sticking with a traditional IRA or converting to a Roth, again, depends on your individual circumstances, including your income, your tax bracket and the amount of deductions you have each year.

Is it better to have a Roth IRA or traditional IRA? It depends on your individual circumstance. Some people don't mind having taxable income from an IRA. Their income might not be very high and their RMD might not bump their tax bracket up, so it's not as big a deal. A similar situation might involve income from Social Security. Social Security benefits are taxed based on other income you are drawing. If you are in a position where none or very little of your Social Security benefit is subject to taxes, paying income tax on your RMD may be very easy.

» *There are also situations where leveraging taxable income from a traditional IRA can work to your advantage come tax time. For example, Miles and Gloria have a dream of buying a boat when they retire. It is something they have looked forward to their entire marriage. In addition to the savings and investments that they created to supply them with income during retirement, which includes a traditional IRA, they have also saved money for the sole purpose of purchasing a boat once they stop working.*

When the time comes and they finally buy the boat of their dreams, they pay an additional $15,000 in sales taxes that year because of the large purchase. Because they are retired and earning less money, the deductions they used to be able to realize from their income taxes are no longer there. The high amount of sales taxes they paid on the boat puts them in a position where they could benefit from taking taxable income from a traditional IRA.

When Miles and Gloria's financial professional learns about their purchase, he immediately contacts a CPA at his firm to run the numbers. They determine that by taking a $15,000 distribution from their IRA, they could fulfill their income needs to offset the $15,000 sales tax deduction that they were claiming due to the purchase of their boat. In the *end, they pay zero taxes on their income distribution from their IRA.*

The moral of the story? **Having a tax diversified landscape gives you options.** Having capital assets that can be liquidated, tax-advantaged income options and sources that can create capital gains or capital losses will put you in a position to play your cards right no matter what you want to accomplish with your taxes. The ace up your sleeve is your financial professional and the CPAs they work with. Do yourself a favor and *plan* your taxes instead of *reporting* them!

CHAPTER 11 CHECKLIST //

- Are you on the lookout for the "free bridge" option in your tax strategy during retirement?
- Have you considered converting from a traditional to a Roth IRA to provide tax-advantaged retirement income? Converting to a Roth IRA can also help you preserve and build your legacy.
- Are you aware of the many ways to reduce your taxes? Being smart about your Roth IRA conversion is one of the main ways to do so.

12

YOUR LEGACY BEYOND DOLLARS AND CENTS

*Who do you think has the best interests of
your beneficiaries in mind?*

When most people think about an estate, it may seem like something only the very wealthy have: a stately manor or an enormous business. But a legacy is something else entirely. A legacy is more than the sum total of the financial assets you have accumulated. It is the lasting impression you make on those you leave behind. The dollar and cents are just a small part of a legacy.

A legacy encompasses the stories that others tell about you, or the shared experiences and values they enjoyed with you during your time here on earth. An estate may pay for college tuition, but a legacy may inform your grandchildren about the importance of higher education and self-reliance.

A legacy may also contain family heirlooms or items of emotional significance. It may be a piece of art your great-grandmother painted, family photos, or a childhood keepsake.

When you go about planning your legacy, certainly explore strategies that can maximize the financial benefit to the ones you care about. But also take the time to ensure that you have organized the whole of your legacy, and let that be a part of the last gift you leave. Many people avoid planning their legacy until they feel they must. Something may change in your life, like the birth of a grandchild, the diagnosis of a serious health problem, or the death of a close friend or loved one. Waiting for tragedy to strike in order to get your affairs in order is not the best course of action. The emotional stress of that kind of situation can make it hard to make patient, thoughtful decisions, and the fact of the matter is that if you don't plan your legacy, someone else will. That someone else is usually a combination of the IRS and other government entities: lawyers, executors, courts, and accountants.

THE BENEFITS OF PLANNING YOUR LEGACY

The distribution of your assets, whether in the form of property, stocks, Individual Retirement Accounts, 401(k)s or liquid assets, can be a complicated undertaking if you haven't left clear instructions about how you want them handled. Not having a plan will cost more money and take more time, leaving your loved ones to wait (sometimes for years) and receive less of your legacy than if you had a clear plan.

Planning your legacy will help your assets be transferred with little delay and little confusion. Instead of leaving decisions about how to distribute your estate to your family, attorneys or financial professionals, preserve your legacy and your wishes by drafting a clear plan at an early age.

And while you know all that, it can still be hard to sit down and do it. It reminds you that life is short, and the relatively complicated nature of sorting through your assets can feel like a daunting task. But one thing is for sure: *it is impossible for your assets to be transferred or distributed the way you want at the end of your life if you don't have a plan.*

Ask yourself:

- Are my assets up to date?
- Have my primary and contingent beneficiaries been clearly designated?
- Does my plan allow for restriction of a beneficiary?
- Does my legacy plan address minor children that I want to provide with income?
- Does my legacy plan allow for multi-generational payout?

Answers to these questions are critical if you want the final say in how your assets are distributed. In order to achieve your legacy goals, you need a plan.

MAKING A PLAN

Eventually, when your income need is filled and you have sufficient standby money to meet your need for emergencies, travel or other extra expenses you are planning for, whatever isn't used during your lifetime becomes your financial legacy. The money that you do not use during your lifetime will either go to loved ones, unloved ones, charity, or the IRS. The questions is, who would you rather disinherit?

By having a legacy plan that clearly outlines your assets, your beneficiaries and your distribution goals, you can make sure that your money and property is ending up in the hands of the people you determine beforehand. Is it really that big of a deal? It absolutely is. Think about it. Without a clear plan, it is impossible for anyone to know if your beneficiary designations are current and reflect your wishes because you haven't clearly expressed who your beneficiaries are. You may have an idea of who you want your assets to go to, but without a plan, it is anyone's guess. It is also impossible to know if the titling of your assets is accurate unless you have gone through and determined whose name is on the titles. More importantly, *if you have not clearly and effectively communicated your desires regarding the planned distribution of your legacy, you and your family may end up losing a large part of it.*

As you can see, managing a legacy is more complicated than having an attorney read your will, divide your estate and write checks to your heirs. The additional issue of taxes, Family Maximum Benefit calculations and a host of other decisions rear their heads. Educating yourself about the best options for positioning your legacy assets is a challenging undertaking. Working with a financial professional who is versed in determining the most efficient and effective ways of preserving and distributing your legacy can save you time, money and strife.

So, how do you begin?

Making a Legacy Plan Starts with a Simple List. The first, and one of the largest, steps to setting up an estate plan with a financial professional that reflects your desires is creating a detailed inventory of your assets and debts (if you have any). You need to know what assets you have, who the beneficiaries are, how much they are worth and how they are titled. You can start by identifying and listing your assets. This is a good starting point for working with a financial professional who can then help you determine the detailed information about your assets that will dictate how they are distributed upon your death.

If you are particularly concerned about leaving your kids and grandkids a lifetime of income with minimal taxes, you will want to discuss a Stretch IRA option with your financial professional.

STRETCH IRAS: GETTING THE MOST OUT OF YOUR MONEY

In 1986, the U.S. Congress passed a law that allows for multi-generational distributions of IRA assets. This type of distribution is called a Stretch IRA because it stretches the distribution of the account out over a longer period of time to several beneficiaries. It also allows the account to continue accumulating value throughout your relatives' lifetimes. You can use a Stretch IRA as an income tool that distributes throughout your lifetime, your children's lifetimes and your grandchildren's lifetimes.

Stretch IRAs are an attractive option for those more concerned with creating income for their loved ones than leaving them with a lump sum that may be subject to a high tax rate. With traditional IRA distributions, non-spousal beneficiaries must generally take distributions from their inherited IRAs, whether transferred or not, within five years after the death of the IRA owner. An exception to this rule applies if the beneficiary elects to take distributions over his or her lifetime, which is referred to as stretching the IRA.

Let's begin by looking at the potential of stretching an IRA throughout multiple generations.

> » In this scenario, Mr. Cleaver has an IRA with a current balance of $350,000. If we assume a five percent annual rate of return, and a 28 percent tax rate, the Stretch IRA turned a $502,625 legacy into more than $1.5 million. Doubling the value of the IRA also provided Mr. Cleaver, his wife, two children and three grandchildren with income. Not choosing the stretch option would have cost nearly $800,000 and had impacts on six of Mr. Cleaver's loved ones.

Unfortunately, many things may also play a role in failing to stretch IRA distributions. It can be tempting for a beneficiary to

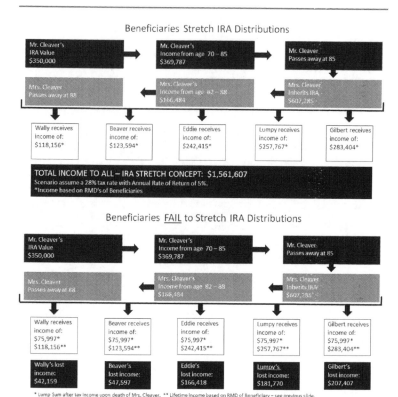

Beneficiaries Stretch IRA Distributions

take a lump sum of money despite the tax consequences. Fortunately, if you want to solidify your plan for distribution, there are options that will allow you to open up an IRA and incorporate "spendthrift" clauses for your beneficiaries. This will ensure your legacy is stretched appropriately and to your specifications. Only certain insurance companies allow this option, and you will not find this benefit with any brokerage accounts. You need to work with a financial professional who has the appropriate relationship with an insurance company that provides this option.

CHAPTER 12 CHECKLIST //

- What is your definition of legacy? Your legacy encompasses more than just the physical assets left behind for your children, grandchildren and charities or organizations. It's how you will be remembered.
- Have you made a legacy planning list?
- Do you have a plan for passing on what you own to your heirs in the most tax efficient way possible? Issues such as taxes, Family Maximum Benefit calculations and a host of other concerns make it necessary to educate yourself. Working with a financial professional can save you time, money and stress.

13

PREPARING YOUR LEGACY

*New investment grade life insurance is not just in case you die.
These policies can provide unparalleled 'Life' benefits while
you are still alive.*

*Sam organized his assets long ago. He and his wife Julie started plan-
ning their retirement early and made investment decisions that would
meet his needs. With a combination of IRA to Roth IRA conversions,
a series of income annuities and a well-planned money management
strategy overseen by his financial professional, he easily filled his
income gap and was able to focus on ways to accumulate his wealth
throughout his retirement. He reorganized his Red Money and Green
Money as he got older. When Sam retired, he had an income plan
created that allowed him to maximize his Social Security benefit. He
even had enough to accumulate wealth during his retirement. At this
point, Sam turned his attention to planning his legacy. He wanted to*

know how he could maximize the amount of his legacy he will pass on to his grandchildren.

Sam met with an attorney to draw up a will, but he quickly learned that while having a will was a good plan, it wasn't the most efficient way to distribute his legacy. In fact, relying solely on a will created several roadblocks.

The two main problems that arose for Sam were *Probate* and *Unintentional Disinheritance:*

Problem #1: Probate

Probate. Just speaking the word out loud can cause shivers to run down your spine. Probate's ugly reputation is well deserved. It can be a costly, time consuming process that diminishes your estate and can delay the distribution of your estate to your loved ones. Nasty stuff, by any measure. Unless you have made a clear legacy plan and discussed options for avoiding probate, it is highly likely that you have many assets that might pass through probate needlessly. ***If your will and beneficiary designations aren't correctly structured, some of these assets will go through the probate process, which can turn dollars into cents.***

If you have a will, probate is usually just a formality. There is little risk that your will won't be executed per your instructions. The problem arises when the costs and lengthy timeline that probate creates come into play. Probate proceedings are notoriously expensive, lengthy and ponderous. A typical probate process identifies all of your assets and debts, pays any taxes and fees that you owe (including estate tax), pays court fees, and distributes your property and assets to your heirs. This process usually takes at least a year, and can take even longer before your heirs actually receive anything that you have left for them. For this reason, and because of the sometimes exorbitant fees that may be charged by lawyers and accountants during the process, probate has earned a nasty reputation. Probate can also be a painstakingly public process. Because the probate process happens in court, the assets you own that go through a probate procedure become part of the public record. While this may not seem like a big deal to some, other people don't want that kind of intimate information available to the public.

Additionally, if your estate is entirely distributed via your will, the money that your family may need to cover the costs of your medical bills, funeral expenses and estate taxes could be tied up in probate, which can last up to a year or more. While immediate family members may have the option of requesting immediate cash from your assets during probate to cover immediate health care expenses, taxes, and fees, that process comes with its own set of complications. Choosing alternative methods for distributing your legacy can make life easier for your loved ones and can help them claim more of your estate in a more timely fashion than traditional methods.

A simpler and less tedious approach is to avoid probate altogether by structuring your estate to be distributed outside of the probate process. Two common ways of doing this are by structuring your assets inside a life insurance plan, and by using individual retirement planning tools like IRAs that give you the option of designating a beneficiary upon your death. In addition, some states now allow for *"Transfer on Death"* deeds and provisions thereby providing you the opportunity to name beneficiaries on non-qualified accounts, your home and personal property.

Problem #2: Unintentionally Disinheriting Your Family

You would never want to unintentionally disinherit a loved one or loved ones because of confusion surrounding your legacy plan. Unfortunately, it happens. Why? This terrible situation is typically caused by a simple lack of understanding. In particular, mistakes regarding legacy distribution occur with regards to those whom people care for the most: their grandchildren.

One of the most important ways to plan for the inheritance of your grandchildren is by properly structuring the distribution of your legacy. Specifically, you need to know if your legacy is going to be distributed *per stirpes* or *per capita*.

Per Stirpes. *Per stirpes* is a legal term in Latin that means "by the branch." Your estate will be distributed *per stirpes* if you designate each branch of your family to receive an equal share of your estate. In the event that your children predecease you, their share will be distributed evenly between their children — your grandchildren.

Per Capita. *Per capita* distribution is different in that you may designate different amounts of your estate to be distributed to members of the same generation.

Per stirpes distribution of assets will follow the family tree down the line as the predecessor beneficiaries pass away. On the other hand, per capita distribution of assets ends on the branch of the family tree with the death of a designated beneficiary. For example, when your child passes away, in a per capita distribution, your grandchildren would not receive distributions from the assets that you designated to your child.

What the terms mean is not nearly as important as what they do, however. The reality is that improperly titled assets could accidentally leave your grandchildren disinherited upon the death of their parents. It's easy to check, and it's even easier to fix.

A simple way to remember the difference between the two types of distribution goes something like this: "***Stirpes are forever and Capita is capped.***"

Another way to avoid complicated legacy distribution problems, and the probate process, is by leveraging a life insurance plan.

LIFE INSURANCE: AN IMPORTANT LEGACY TOOL

One of the most powerful legacy tools you can leverage is a good life insurance policy. Life insurance is a highly efficient legacy tool because it creates money when it is needed or desired the most. Over the years, life insurance has become less expensive, while it offers more features, and it provides longer guarantees.

There are many unique benefits of life insurance that can help your beneficiaries get the most out of your legacy. Some of them include:

- Providing beneficiaries with a tax-free, liquid asset.
- Covering the costs associated with your death.
- Providing income for your dependents.
- Offering an investment opportunity for your beneficiaries.
- Covering expenses such as tuition or mortgage down payments for your children or grandchildren.

Very few people want life insurance, but nearly everyone wants what it does. Life insurance is specifically, and uniquely, capable of creating money when it is needed most. When a loved one passes, no amount of money can remove the pain of loss. And certainly, money doesn't solve the challenges that might arise with losing someone important.

It has been said that when you have money, you have options. When you don't have money, your options are severely limited. You might imagine a life insurance policy can give your family and loved ones options that would otherwise be impossible.

» *Luke spent the last 20 years building a small business. In so many ways, it is a family business. Each of his three children, Zoe, Emma and Zach, worked in the shop part-time during high school, and his wife, Emily, helped with the books. But after all three kids attended college and moved on to start their lives, only Emma returned to join her father. After*

Luke's wife passed away, it hit him that Emma would be the one to run the business full-time.

Luke is able to retire comfortably on Social Security and on-going income from the shop, but the business represents to him his legacy. To be fair, however, he wants to leave an equal legacy to each of his other two children. There is no simple way to divide the business into thirds and still leave the business intact for Emma.

Luke ends up buying a life insurance policy to make up the difference. Zoe and Zach will receive their share of an inheritance in cash from the life insurance policy and Emma will be able to inherit the business intact.

Luke is able to accomplish all his goals, treat all three children equitably and leave Emma the business she helped to build.

If you have a life insurance policy but you haven't looked at it in a while, you may not know how it operates, how much it is worth and how it will be distributed to your beneficiaries. You may also need to update your beneficiaries on your policy. In short, without a comprehensive review of your policy, you don't really know where the money will go or to whom it will go.

If you don't have a life insurance policy but are looking for options to maintain and grow your legacy, speaking with a professional can show you the benefits of life insurance. Many people don't consider buying a life insurance policy until some event in their life triggers it, like the loss of a loved one, an accident or a health condition.

BENEFITS OF LIFE INSURANCE

Life insurance is a useful and secure tool for contingency planning, ensuring that your dependents receive the assets that you want them to have, and for meeting the financial goals you have set for the future. While it bears the name "Life Insurance," it is, in reality, a diverse financial tool that can meet many needs. The main function of a life insurance policy is to provide financial assets for your survivors. Life insurance is particularly efficient at achieving this goal because it provides a tax-advantaged lump sum of money in the form of a death benefit to your beneficiary or beneficiaries. That financial asset can be used in a number of ways. It can be structured as an investment to provide income for your spouse or children, it can pay down debts, and it can be used to cover estate taxes and other costs associated with death.

Living Benefits:

Many of today's life insurance policies and annuity products also have riders and provisions for increased income in the event of chronic illness. Often known as Life Benefits, these products provide you with the means to pay for home health care or a nursing home facility while you are still alive. With annuities, these benefits are sometimes known as "income doublers" because the fixed income contracted by the rider will double should you or your spouse require long term care. Long term care can include basic custodial services such as cleaning and taking out the garbage, or it can be more involved and include intrinsic nursing services. Even if it's too late to qualify for traditional long term care insurance, long term care riders on annuity and life insurance products might still be an option for you, and if you never need long term care, that money is not lost. Instead, your beneficiaries receive a legacy.

In addition, Investment Grade life insurance can provide you with tax-free free retirement income while you are alive.

Tax Benefits:

Tax liabilities on the estate you leave behind are inevitable. Capital property, for instance, is taxed at its fair market value at the time of your death, unless that property is transferred to your spouse. If the property has appreciated during the time you owned it, taxation on capital gains will occur. Registered Retirement Savings Plans (RRSPs) and other similarly structured assets are also included as taxable income unless transferred to a beneficiary as well. Those are just a few examples of how an estate can become subject to a heavy tax burden. The unique benefits of a life insurance policy provide ways to handle this tax burden, solving any liquidity problems that may arise if your family members want to hold onto an illiquid asset, such as a piece of property or an investment. Life insurance can provide a significant amount of money to a family member or other beneficiary, and that money is likely to remain exempt from taxation or seizure.

Protection Benefits:
One of life insurance's most important benefits is that it is not considered part of the estate of the policy holder. The death benefit that is paid by the insurance company goes exclusively to the beneficiaries listed on the policy. This shields the proceeds of the policy from fees and costs that can reduce an estate, including probate proceedings, attorneys' fees and claims made by creditors. The distribution of your life insurance policy is also unaffected by delays of the estate's distribution, like probate. Your beneficiaries will get the proceeds of the policy in a timely fashion, regardless of how long it takes for the rest of your estate to be settled.

Investing a portion of your assets in a life insurance policy can also protect that portion of your estate from creditors. If you owe money to someone or some entity at the time of your death, a creditor is not able to claim any money from a life insurance policy or an annuity, for that matter. An exception to this rule would be if you had already used the life insurance policy as collateral against a loan. If a large portion of the money you want to dedicate to your legacy is sitting in a savings account, investment or other liquid form, creditors may be able to receive their claim on it before your beneficiaries get anything; that is, if there's anything left. A life insurance policy protects your assets from creditors and ensures that your beneficiaries get the money that you intend them to have.

HOW MUCH LIFE INSURANCE DO YOU NEED?

Determining the type of policy and the amount right for you depends on an analysis of your needs. A financial professional can help you complete a needs analysis that will highlight the amount of insurance that you require to meet your goals. This type of personalized review will allow you to determine ways to continue providing income for your spouse or any dependents you may have. A financial professional can also help you calculate the amount of income that your policy should replace to meet the needs of your beneficiaries and the duration of the distribution of that income.

You may also want to use your life insurance policy to meet any expenses associated with your death. These can include funeral costs, fees from probate and legal proceedings, and taxes. You may also want to dedicate a portion of your policy proceeds to help fund tuition or other expenses for your children or grandchildren. You can buy a policy and hope it covers all of those costs, or you can work with a professional who can calculate exactly how much insurance you need and how to structure it to meet your goals. Which would you rather do?

AVOIDING POTENTIAL SNAGS

There are benefits to having life insurance supersede the direction given in a will or other estate plan, but there are also some potential snags that you should address to meet your wishes. For example, if your will instructs that your assets be divided equally between your two children but your life insurance beneficiary is listed as just one of the children, the assets in the life insurance policy will only be distributed to the child listed as the beneficiary. The beneficiary designation of your life insurance supersedes your will's instruction. This is important to understand when designating beneficiaries on a policy you purchase. Work with a professional to make sure that your beneficiaries are accurately listed on your assets, especially your life insurance policies.

USING LIFE INSURANCE TO BUILD YOUR LEGACY

Depending on your goals, there are strategies you can use that could multiply how much you leave behind. Life insurance is one of the most surefire and efficient investment tools for building a substantial legacy that will meet your financial goals.

Here is a brief overview of how life insurance can boost your legacy:

- Life insurance provides an immediate increase in your legacy.
- It provides an income tax-advantaged death benefit for your beneficiaries.
- A good life insurance policy has the opportunity to accumulate value over time.
- It may have an option to include long-term care (LTC) or chronic illness benefits should you require them.

If your Green Money income needs for retirement are met, you may have extra assets that you want to earmark as legacy funds. By electing to invest those assets into a life insurance policy, you can immediately increase the amount of your legacy. Remember, **life insurance allows you to transfer a tax-advantaged lump sum of money to your beneficiaries. It remains in your control during your lifetime, can provide for your long-term care needs and bypasses probate costs.** And make no mistake, taxes can have a huge impact on your legacy. Not only that, income and assets from your legacy can have tax implications for your beneficiaries, as well.

Here's a brief overview of how taxes could affect your legacy and your beneficiaries:

- The higher your income, the higher the rate at which it is taxed.
- Withdrawals from qualified plans are taxed as income.
- What's more, when you leave a large qualified plan, it ends up being taxed at a high rate.
- If you left a $500,000 IRA to your child, they could end up owing as much as $140,000 in income taxes.
- However, if you could just withdraw $50,000 a year, the tax bill might only be $10,000 per year.

How could you use that annual amount to leave a larger legacy? Luckily, you can leverage a life insurance policy to avoid those tax penalties, preserving a larger amount of your legacy and freeing your beneficiaries from an added tax burden.

> *When Jenna turned 70 years old, she decided it was time to look into life insurance policy options. She still feels young, but she wants to plan ahead so she can pass on some of her legacy to her grandchildren. They have become a close family, and Jenna wants to be remembered when she goes.*

> *Jenna doesn't really want to think about life insurance, but she does want the security, reliability and tax-advantaged distribution that it offers. She lives modestly with her new husband, Paul. Their combined Social Security benefits and his income producing assets meet all their income needs. As the beneficiary of her late husband's life insurance policy, she has $100,000 in an account that she does not want to spend down, and she doesn't anticipate ever needing since her income needs are currently met.*

*After looking at several different investment options with a professional, Jenna decides that a Single Premium life insurance policy fits her needs best. She can buy the policy with a $100,000 one-time payment and she is guaranteed that it would provide more than the value of the contract to her beneficiaries. If she left the money in the CD, it would be subject to taxes. But for every dollar that she puts into the life insurance policy, her beneficiaries are guaranteed at least that dollar plus a death benefit, and all of it will be **tax-free!***

For $100,000, Jenna's particular policy offers a $170,000 death benefit distribution to her beneficiaries. By moving the $100,000 from a CD to a life insurance policy, Jenna increases her legacy by 70 percent. Not only that, she has also sheltered it from taxes, so her beneficiaries will be able to receive $1.70 for every $1.00 that she entered into the policy!

While buying the policy doesn't allow her to use the money for herself, it does allow her family to benefit from her well-planned legacy.

MAKE YOUR WISHES KNOWN

Estate taxes used to be a much hotter topic in the mid-2000s when the estate tax limits and exclusions were much smaller and taxed at a higher rate than today. In 2008, estates valued at $2 million or more were taxed at 45 percent. Just two years later, the limit was raised to $5 million dollars taxed at 35 percent. The limit has continued to rise ever since. The limit applies to fewer people than before. Estate organization, however, is just as important as ever, and it affects everyone.

Ask yourself:

• Are your assets actually titled and held the way you think they are?

• Are your beneficiaries set up the way you think they should be?

- Have there been changes to your family or those you desire as beneficiaries?

There is more to your legacy beyond your property, money, investments and other assets that you leave to family members, loved ones and charities. Everyone has a legacy beyond money. You also leave behind personal items of importance, your values and beliefs, your personal and family history, and your wishes. Beyond a will and a plan for your assets, it is important that you make your wishes known to someone for the rest of your personal legacy. When it comes time for your family and loved ones to make decisions after you are gone, knowing your wishes can help them make decisions that honor you and your legacy, and give meaning to what you leave behind. Your professional can help you organize.

Think about your:
- Personal stories / recollections
- Values
- Personal items of emotional significance
- Financial assets

Do you want to make a plan to pass these things on to your family?

WORKING WITH A PROFESSIONAL

Part of using life insurance to your greatest advantage is selecting the policy and provider that can best meet your goals. Venturing into the jungle of policies, brokers and salespeople can be overwhelming, and can leave you wondering if you've made the best decision. Working with a trusted financial professional can help you cut through the red tape, the "sales-speak" and confusion to find a policy that meets your goals and best serves your desires for your money. If you already have a policy, a financial professional can help you review it and become familiar with the policy's premium, the guarantees the policy affords, its performance, and its features and benefits. A financial professional can also help you make any necessary changes to the policy.

» *When Irene turned 88, her neighbor, Louise, finally convinced her to meet with a financial professional to help her organize her assets and get her legacy in order. Although Irene is reluctant to let a stranger in on her personal finances, she ends up very glad that she did.*

In the process of listing Irene's assets and her beneficiaries, her professional finds a man's name listed as the beneficiary of an old life insurance annuity that she owns. It turns out, the man is Irene's ex-husband who is still alive. Had Irene passed away before her ex-husband, the annuities and any death benefits that came with them, would have been passed on to her ex-husband. This does not reflect her latest wishes.

Things change, relationships evolve and the way you would like your legacy organized needs to adapt to the changes that happen throughout your life. There may be a new child or grandchild in your family, or you may have been divorced or remarried. A professional will regularly review your legacy assets and ask you questions to make sure that everything is up to date and that the current organization reflects your current wishes.

CHAPTER 13 CHECKLIST //

- Have you met with an estate planning attorney to prepare your legacy? Legacy planning tools include the creation of a will, trusts, living will, and durable power of attorney for health care considerations.
- Have you reviewed your current life insurance policies in order to determine if restructuring your life insurance makes sense?
- Are you aware of the Life benefits that today's life insurance policies can provide? Life insurance provides for the distribution of tax-free, liquid assets to your beneficiaries and can significantly build your legacy in addition to helping you pay for the high costs of medical care while you are still living.
- Have you considered the use of life insurance as a tool to provide you tax-free retirement income?
- Are you working with a financial professional to help you select the life insurance policy that best fits your needs?

14

CHOOSING A FINANCIAL PROFESSIONAL

From the moment you dip your toes into the retirement planning pool to the point you start swimming laps, your assets organized, your income needs met, and your accumulation and legacy plans in place, working with a professional that you trust can make all the difference in how well your retirement reflects your desires.

It is important to know what you are looking for before taking the plunge. There are many people that would love to handle your money, but not everyone is qualified to handle it in a way that leads to a holistic approach to creating a solid retirement plan.

The distinction being made here is that you should look for someone that puts your interests first and actively wants to help you meet your goals and objectives. Oftentimes, the products someone sells you matter less than their dedication to making sure that you have a plan that meets your needs.

Professionals take your whole financial position into consideration. They make plans that adjust your risk exposure, invest in tools that secure your desired income during retirement and create investment strategies that allow you to continue accumulating wealth during your retirement for you to use later or to contribute to your legacy. If you buy stocks or mutual funds with a broker, use a different agent for a life insurance policy and have an unmanaged 401(k) through your employer, working with a financial professional will consolidate the management of your assets so you have one trustworthy person quarterbacking all of the team elements of your portfolio. Financial products and investment tools change, but the concepts that lie behind wise retirement planning are lasting. In the end, a financial professional's approach is designed for those serious about planning for retirement. *Can you say the same thing about the person that advises you about your financial life?*

It's easy to see how choosing a financial professional can be one of the most important decisions you can make in your life. Not only do they provide you with advice, they also manage the personal assets that supply your retirement income and contribute to your legacy. So, how do you find a good one?

HOW TO FIND A FINANCIAL PROFESSIONAL YOU CAN TRUST

Taking care to select a financial professional is one of the best things you can do for yourself and for your future. Your professional has influence and control of your investment decisions, making their role in your life more than just important. Your financial security and the quality of your retirement depends on the decisions, investment strategies and asset structuring that you and your professional create.

Working with a professional is different than calling up a broker when you want to buy or trade some stock. This isn't a decision that you can hand off to anyone else. You need to bring your time and attention to the table when it comes to finding someone with whom you can entrust your financial life. Separating the wheat from the chaff will take some work, but you'll be happy you did it.

While no one can tell you exactly who to choose or how to choose them, the following information can help you narrow the field:

- You can start by asking your friends, family and colleagues for referrals. You will want to pay particular attention to the recommendations that you get from others who are in your similar financial situation and who have similar lifestyle choices. The professional for the CEO of your company may have a different skill-set than the skill-set of the professional befitting your cousin who has 3 kids and a Subaru like you. Do follow-up research on the Internet as well. Look up the people who have been recommended to you on websites like LinkedIn that show the work history, referrals and experience of the candidates that you find most attractive. You will also learn about the firms with or for whom they work. The investment philosophies and reputations of the companies they work for will tell you a lot about how they will handle your money.

- The other side of the coin, however, is that everyone and their brother has a recommendation about how you should manage your money and who should manage it for you. From hot stock tips to "the best money manager in the state," people love to share good information that makes them look like they are in-the-know. Nobody wants to talk about the bad stock purchases they made, the times they lost money and the poor selections they made regarding financial professionals or stock brokers. If you decide to take a friend or family member's recommendation, make sure they have a substantial, long-term experience with the financial professional and that their glowing review isn't just based on a one-time "win."

- You can also use online tools like the search function of the Financial Planning Association (http://www.fpanet. org/) and the National Association of Personal Financial professionals (http://www.napfa.org/). Most of the professionals listed on these sites do not earn commissions from selling financial products, but are instead paid on a fee-only basis for their services. It is important to understand how your professional is being paid. It is generally considered preferable to work with a fee-based professional who will not have conflicts of interests between earning a commission and acting in your best interests.

- Many professionals may also be brokers or dealers that can earn commissions on things like life insurance, certain types of annuities and disability insurance. These professionals have most likely intentionally overlapped their roles so that if their clients choose to purchase insurance or investment products that require a broker or dealer, those clients won't have to find an additional person to work with. Again, understanding the role of your professional will help you make your determination.

NARROWING THE FIELD

1. Decide on the Type of Professional with Whom You Want to Work. There are four basic kinds of financial professionals. Many professionals may play overlapping roles. It is important to know a professional's primary function, how they charge for their services and whether they are obligated to act in your best interest.

Registered representatives, better known as stockbrokers or bank / investment representatives, make their living by earning commissions on insurance products and investment services. Stockbrokers basically sell you things. The products from which they make the highest commission are sometimes the products that they recommend to their clients. If you want to make a simple transaction, such as buying or selling a particular stock, a registered representative can help you. Although registered representatives are licensed professionals, if you want to create a structured and planful approach to positioning your assets for retirement, you might want to consider continuing your search.

The term "planner" is often misused. It can refer to credible professionals that are CPAs, CFPs and ChFCs to your uncle's next door neighbor who claims to have a lead on some undervalued stock about to be "discovered." A wide array of people may claim to be planners because there are no requirements to be a planner. The term financial planner, however, refers to someone who is properly registered as an investment advisor and serves as a fiduciary as described below.

Financial professionals are the diamonds in the rough. These Registered Investment Advisors are compensated on a fee basis. They do, however, often have licensure as stockbrokers or insurance agents, allowing them to earn commissions on certain transactions. More importantly, **financial professionals are financial fiduciaries, meaning they are required to make financial decisions in your best interest and reflecting your risk tolerance.** Investment Advisors are held to high ethical standards and are highly regarded in the financial industry. Financial professionals also often take a more comprehensive approach to asset management. These professionals are trained and credentialed to plan and coordinate their clients' assets in order to meet their goals or retirement and legacy planning. They are not focused on individual stocks, investments or markets. They look at the big picture, the whole enchilada.

Money managers are on par with financial professionals. However, they are often given explicit permission to make investment decisions without advanced approval by their clients.

Understanding who you are working with and what their title is the first step to planning your retirement. While each of the above-mentioned types of financial professionals can help you with aspects of your finances, it is **financial professionals** who have the most intimate role, the most objective investment strategies and the most unbiased mode of compensation for their services. A financial professional can also help you with the non-financial aspects of your legacy and can help you find ways to create a tax planning strategy to help you save money.

2. Be Objective. At the end of the day, you need to separate the weak from the strong. While you might want a strong personal rapport with your professional, or you may want to choose your professional for their personality and positive attitude, it is more important that you find someone who will give sage advice regarding achieving your retirement goals.

It can be helpful to use a process of elimination to narrow the field of potential professionals. Look into five or six potential leads and cross off your list the ones that don't meet your requirements until only one or two remain. Cross-check your remaining choices against the list of things you need from a professional. Make sure they represent a firm that has the investment tools and products that you desire, and make sure they have experience in retirement planning. That is, after all, the main goal.

Don't be afraid to investigate each of your candidates. You'll want to ask the same questions and look for the same information from everyone you consider so you can then compare them and discern which is best for you. You'll want to take a look at the specific credentials of each professional, their experience and competence, their ethics and fiduciary status, their history and track record, and a list of the services that they offer. The professionals who meet all or most of your qualifications are the ones you will contact for an interview.

Potential professionals should meet your qualifications in the following categories:

- *Credentials:* Look at their experience, the quality of their education, any associations to which they belong and certifications they have earned. Someone who has continued their professional education through ongoing certifications will be more up-to-date on current financial practices compared to someone who got their degree 25 years ago and hasn't done a thing since.

- *Practices:* Look at the track record of your candidates, how they are compensated for their services, the reports and analysis they offer, and their value added services.

- *Services:* Your professional must meet your needs. If you are planning your retirement, you should work with someone who offers services that help you to that end. You want someone who can offer planning, advice on investment strategies, ways to calculate risk, advice on insurance and annuities products, and ways to manage your tax strategy.

- *Ethics:* You want to work with someone who is above board and does things the right way. Vet them by checking their compliance record, current licensing, fiduciary status and, yes, even their criminal record. You never know!

3. Ask for and Check References. Once you have selected two or three professionals that you want to meet, call or email them and ask for references. Every professional should be able to provide you with at least two or three names. In fact, they will probably be eager to share them with you. Most professionals rely on references for validation of their success, quality of services and likability. You should, however, take them with a grain of salt. You have no way to know whether or not references are a professional's friends or colleagues.

It is worth contacting references, however, to check for inconsistencies. Ask each reference the same set of questions to get the same basic information. How long have they been working with the professional? What kind of services have they used and were they happy with them? What type of financial planning did they use the professional for? Were they versed in the type of financial planning that you needed? You can also ask them direct questions to elicit candid responses. What was the full cost of the expenses that your professional charged you? Do the reports and statements you receive come from the same firm? Questions like these can help you get a sense of how well the reference knows their professional and whether or not they are a quality reference.

A good reference is a bit like icing on the cake. It's nice to have them, but nothing speaks louder than a good track record and quality experience. And remember that a good reference, while nice to hear, is relatively cheap. How many times have you heard someone on the golf course or at work telling you how great their stockbroker is? But how many times have you heard about the bad investments or losses they have experienced?

HOW TO INTERVIEW CANDIDATES

After vetting your candidates and narrowing down a list of professionals that you think might be a good fit for you, it's time to start interviewing.

When you meet in person with a professional, you want to take advantage of your time with them. The presentations and information that they share with you will be important to pay attention to, but you will also want to control some aspects of the interview. After a professional has told you what they want you to hear, it's time to ask your own questions to get the specific information you need to make your decision.

Make sure to prepare a list of questions and an informal agenda so that you can keep track of what you want to ask and what points you want the professional to touch on during the interview. Using the same questions and agenda will also allow you to more easily compare the professionals after you have interviewed them all. Remember that these interviews are just that, *interviews*. You are meeting with several professionals to determine with whom you want to work. Don't agree to anything or sign anything during an interview until after you have made your final decision.

It can also be helpful to put a time limit on your interviews and to meet the professionals at their offices. The time limit will keep things on track and will allow structured time for presentations and questions/discussion. By meeting them at their office, you can get a sense of the work environment, the staff culture and attitude, and how the firm does business. If you are unable to travel to a professional's office and must meet them at your home or office, make sure that your interviews are scheduled with plenty of time between so the professionals don't cross each other's paths.

You can use the following questions during an initial interview to get an understanding of how each professional does business and whether they are a good fit for you:

1. How do you charge for your services? How much do you charge? This information should be easy to find on their website, but if you don't see it, ask. Find out if they charge an initial planning fee, if they charge a percentage for assets under their management and if they make money by selling specific financial products or services. If so, you should follow up by asking how much the service costs. This will give you an idea of how they really make their money and if they have incentive to sell certain products over others. Make sure you understand exactly how you will be charged so there are no surprises down the road if you decide to work with this person.

2. What are your credentials, licenses, and certifications? There are Certified Financial Planners (CFPs), Chartered Financial Consultants (ChFCs), Investment Advisor Representatives, Certified Public Accountants (CPAs) and Personal Financial Specialists (PFSs). Whatever their credentials or titles, you want to be sure that the professional you work with is an expert in the field relevant to your circumstances. If you want someone to manage your money, you will most likely look for an Investment Advisor. Someone that works with an independent firm will likely have a team of CPAs, CFPs and other financial experts upon whom they can draw. If you like the professional you are meeting with and you think they might be a good fit, but they don't have the accounting experience you want them to have, ask about their firm and the resources available to them. If they work closely with CPAs that are experienced in your needs, it could be a good match.

3. What are the financial services that you and your firm provide? The question within the question here is, "Can you help me achieve my goals?" Some people can only provide you with investment advice, and others are tax consultants. You will likely want to work with someone that provides a complete suite of financial planning services and products that touch on retirement planning, insurance options, legacy and estate structuring, and tax planning. Whatever services they provide, make sure they meet your needs and your anticipated needs.

4. What kinds of clients do you work with the most? A lot of financial professionals work within a niche: retirement planning, risk assessment, life insurance, etc. Finding someone who works with other people that are in the same financial boat as you and who have similar goals can be an important way to make sure they understand your needs. While someone might be a crackerjack annuities cowboy, you might not be interested in that option. Ask follow-up questions that will really help you understand where their expertise lies and whether or not their experience lines up with your needs.

5. May I see a sample of one of your financial plans? You wouldn't buy a car without test driving it, and you should not work with a professional without seeing a sample of how they do business. While there is no formal structure that a financial plan has to follow, the variation between professionals can help you find someone who "speaks your language." One professional may provide you with an in-depth analysis that relies heavily on info graphics and diagrams. Someone else may give you a seven page review of your assets and general recommendations. By seeing a sample plan, you can narrow down who presents information in the way that you desire and in ways that you understand.

6. How do you approach investing? You may be entirely in the dark about how to approach your investments, or you might have some guiding principles. Either way, ask each candidate what their philosophy is. Some will resonate with you and some won't. A good professional who has a realistic approach to investing won't promise you the moon or tell you that they can make you a lot of money. Professionals who are successful at retirement planning and full service financial management will tell you that they will listen to your goals, risk tolerance and comfort level with different types of investment strategies. Working with someone that you trust is critical, and this question in particular can help you find out who you can and who you can't.

7. How do you remain in contact with your clients? Does your prospective professional hold annual, quarterly or monthly meetings? How often do *you* want to meet with your professional? Some people want to check in once a year, go over everything and make sure their ducks are all in a row. If any changes over the previous year or additions to their legacy planning strategy came up, they'll do it on that date. Other people want a monthly update to be more involved in the decision making process and to understand what's happening with their portfolio. You basically need to determine the right degree of involvement for both you and your financial professional. You'll also want to feel out how your professional communicates. Do you prefer phone calls or face-to-face meetings? Do you want your professional to explain things to you in detail or to summarize for you what decisions they've made? Is the professional willing to give you their direct phone number or their email address? More importantly, do you want that information and do you want to be able to contact them in those ways?

8. Are you my main contact, or do you work with a team? This is another way of finding out how involved with you your professional will be, and how often they will meet with you. It is also a way to discover how the firm they represent operates and manages their clients. Some professionals will answer their own phone, meet with you regularly and have your home phone number on speed dial. Others will meet with you once a year and have a partner or assistant check in with you every quarter to give you an update. Other companies take an entirely team-based approach whereby clients have a main contact but their portfolio is handled by a team of professionals that represent the firm. One way isn't better than another, but one way will be best for you. Find out how the professional you are interviewing operates before entering into an agreement.

9. How do you provide a unique experience for your clients? This is a polite way of asking, "Why should I work with you?" A professional should have a compelling answer to this question that connects with you. Their answer will likely touch on their investment philosophy, their communication style and their expertise. If you hear them describing strengths and philosophies that resonate with you, keep them on your list. Some professionals will tell you that they will make investments with your money that match your values, others will say they will maximize your returns and others will say they will protect your capital while structuring your assets for income. Whatever you're looking for in a professional, you will most likely find it in the answer to this question.

This last question you will want to ask *yourself* after you've met with someone who you are considering hiring:

10. Did they ask questions and show signs that they were interested in working with me? A professional who will structure your assets to reflect your risk tolerance and to position you for a comfortable retirement must be a good listener. You will want to pass by a professional who talks non-stop and tells you what to do without listening to what you want them to do. If you felt they listened well and understood your needs, and seemed interested and experienced in your situation, then they might be right for you.

THE IMPORTANCE OF INDEPENDENCE

Not all investment firms and financial professionals are created equal. The information in this book has systematically shown that leveraging investments for income and accumulation in today's market requires new ideas and modern planning. In short, you need innovative ideas to come up with the creative solutions that will provide you with the retirement that you want. Innovation thrives on independence. No matter how good a financial professional is, the firm that they represent needs to operate on principles that make sense in today's economy. Remember, advice about money has been around forever. Good advice, however, changes with the times.

Timing the market, relying on the sale of stocks for income and banking on high treasury and bond returns are not strategies. They aren't even realistic ways to make money or to generate income. Working with an independent agent can help you break free from the old ways of thinking and position you to create a realistic retirement plan.

Working with an independent professional who relies on fee-based income tied to the success of their performance will also give you greater peace of mind. When you do well, they do well, and that's the way it should be. Your independent financial professional will make sure that:

- Your assets are organized and structured to reflect your risk tolerance.
- Your assets will be available to you when you need them and in the way that you need them.
- You will have a lifetime income that will support your lifestyle through your retirement.
- You are handling your taxes as efficiently as possible.
- Your legacy is in order.
- Your Red Money is turned into Yellow or Orange Money, and is managed in your best interest.

» *Remember Jeff and Kim who were comparing their retirement to that of their parents? Their parents got a party and a regular pension check while they had to rely on the savings they'd accumulated in multiple 401(k) accounts.*

Before they met with a financial professional, they had no idea what their retirement would look like.

After they met with a financial professional, they knew exactly what types of assets they had, how much they were worth, how much risk they were exposed to and how they were going to be distributed. They also created an income plan so that they could pay their bills every month the moment they retired, and they maximized their Social Security benefit by targeting the year and month they would get the most lifetime benefits. After their income needs were met, they were able to continue accumulating wealth by investing their extra assets to serve them in the future and contribute to their legacy. Their professional also helped them make decisions that impacted their taxes, protecting the value of their assets and allowing them to keep more of their money.

*This isn't a fairy tale scenario. This is an example of how much you stand to gain by meeting with a financial professional who can help you create a planful approach to your retirement. The concept of Know So and Hope So didn't just apply to their money, it also applied to Jeff and Kim. They **hoped** that they would have enough for retirement and that they had worked hard enough and saved enough to maintain their lifestyle. Working with a financial professional allowed them to **know** that their income needs were secured and structured to provide them with income for the rest of their lives and with some money to spare.*

Now, ask yourself: Is your retirement built on hopes and dreams, or a solid, predictable plan?

IT'S WORTH IT!

Finding, interviewing and selecting a financial professional can seem like a daunting task. And honestly, it will take a good amount of work to narrow the field and find the one you want. In the end, it is worth the blood, sweat and tears. Your retirement, lifestyle, assets and legacy is on the line. The choices you make today will have lasting impacts on your life and the life of your loved ones. Working with someone you trust and know you can rely on to make decisions that will benefit you is invaluable. The work it takes to find them is something you will never regret.

Here is a recap of why working with a financial professional is the best retirement decision you can make:

CHAPTER 14 CHECKLIST //

- Do you have a financial professional who puts your needs first? Your risk tolerance, goals, objectives, needs, wants, liquidity concerns and timeline worries should be the focus of the meeting before they try to sell you any products.
- Have you asked your family and friends for referrals? Make sure to do your due diligence and check out the references of anyone who is recommended to you.
- Have you interviewed candidates to understand how they charge for their services? Did you look for credentials, licenses and certifications? Ask questions such as: How often do you check in with your clients? May I see a sample of one of your financial plans? And, How do you approach investing? These questions will help ensure that you and your professional are a good fit for each other.

GLOSSARY

ANNUAL RESET *(ANNUAL RATCHET, CLIQUET)* – Crediting methods measuring index movement over a one year period. Positive interest is calculated and credited at the end of each contract year and cannot be lost if the index subsequently declines. Say that the index increased from 100 to 110 in one year and the indexed annuity had an 80 percent participation rate. The insurance company would take the 10 percent gross index gain for the year (110-100/100), apply the participation rate (10 percent index gain x 80 percent rate) and credit 8 percent interest to the annuity. But, what if in the following year the index declined back to 100? The individual would keep the 8 percent interest earned and simply receive zero interest for the down year. An annual reset structure preserves credited gains and treats negative index periods as years with zero growth.

ANNUITANT – The person, usually the annuity owner, whose life expectancy is used to calculate the income payment amount on the annuity.

ANNUITY – An annuity is a contract issued by an insurance company that often serves as a type of savings plan used by individuals looking for long term growth and protection of assets that will likely be needed within retirement.

AVERAGING – Index values may either be measured from a start point to an end point (point-to-point) or values between the start point and end point may be averaged to determine an ending value. Index values may be averaged over the days, weeks, months or quarters of the period.

BENEFICIARY – A beneficiary is the person designated to receive payments due upon the death of the annuity owner or the annuitant themselves.

BONUS RATE – A bonus rate is the "extra" or "additional" interest paid during the first year (the initial guarantee period), typically used as an added incentive to get consumers to select their annuity policy over another.

CALL OPTION *(ALSO SEE PUT OPTION)* – Gives the holder the right to buy an underlying security or index at a specified price on or before a given date.

CAP – The maximum interest rate that will be credited to the annuity for the year or period. The cap usually refers to the maximum interest credited after applying the participation rate or yield spread. If the index methodology showed a 20 percent increase, the participation rate was 60 percent and the maximum interest cap was 10 percent, the contract would credit 10 percent interest. A few annuities use a maximum gain cap instead of a maximum interest cap with the participation rate or yield spread applied to the lesser of the gain or the cap. If the index methodology showed a 20 percent increase, the participation rate was 60 percent and the maximum gain cap was 10 percent, the contract would credit 6 percent interest.

COMPOUND INTEREST – Interest is earned on both the original principal and on previously earned interest. It is more favorable than simple interest. Suppose that your original principal was $1 and your interest rate was 10 percent for five years. With simple interest, your value is ($1 + $0.10 interest each year) = $1.50. With compound interest, your value is ($1 x 1.10 x 1.10 x 1.10 x 1.10 x 1.10) = $1.61. The advantage of compound interest over simple interest becomes greater as each subsequent period passes.

CREDITING METHOD *(ALSO SEE METHODOLOGY)* – The formula(s) used to determine the excess interest that is credited above the minimum interest guarantee.

DEATH BENEFITS – The payment the annuity owner's estate or beneficiaries will receive if he or she dies before the annuity matures. On most annuities, this is equal to the current account value. Some annuities offer an enhanced value at death via an optional rider that has a monthly or annual fee associated with it.

EXCESS INTEREST – Interest credited to the annuity contract above the minimum guaranteed interest rate. In an indexed annuity the excess interest is determined by applying a stated crediting method to a specific index or indices.

FIXED ANNUITY – A contract issued by an insurance company guaranteeing a minimum interest rate with the crediting of excess interest determined by the performance of the insurer's general account. Index annuities are fixed annuities.

FIXED DEFERRED ANNUITY – With fixed annuities, an insurance company offers a guaranteed interest rate plus safety of your principal and earnings ((subject to the claims-paying ability of the insurance company). Your interest rate will be reset periodically, based on economic and other factors, but is guaranteed to never fall below a certain rate.

FREE WITHDRAWALS – Withdrawals that are free of surrender charges.

INDEX – The underlying external benchmark upon which the crediting of excess interest is based, also a measure of the prices of a group of securities.

IRA *(INDIVIDUAL RETIREMENT ACCOUNT)* – An IRA is a tax-advantaged personal savings plan that lets an individual set aside money for retirement. All or part of the participant's contributions may be tax deductible, depending on the type of IRA chosen and the participant's personal financial circumstances. Distributions from many employer-sponsored retirement plans may be eligible to be rolled into an IRA to continue tax-deferred growth until the funds are needed. An annuity can be used as an IRA; that is, IRA funds can be used to purchase an annuity.

IRA ROLLOVER – IRA rollover is the phrase used when an individual who has a balance in an employer-sponsored retirement plan transfers that balance into an IRA. Such an exchange, when properly handled, is a tax-advantaged transaction.

LIQUIDITY – The ease with which an asset is convertible to cash. An asset with high liquidity provides flexibility, in that the owner can easily convert it to cash at any time, but it also tends to decrease profitability.

MARKET RISK – The risk of the market value of an asset fluctuating up or down over time. In a fixed or fixed indexed annuity, the original principal and credited interest are not subject to market risk. Even if the index declines, the annuity owner would receive no less than their original principal back if they decided to cash in the policy at the end of the surrender period. Unlike a security, indexed annuities guarantee the original premium and the premium is backed by, and is as safe as, the insurance company that issued it (subject to the claims-paying ability of the insurance company).

METHODOLOGY *(ALSO SEE CREDITING METHOD)* – The way that interest crediting is calculated. On fixed indexed annuities, there are a variety of different methods used to determine how index movement becomes interest credited.

MINIMUM GUARANTEED RETURN *(MINIMUM INTEREST RATE)* – Fixed indexed annuities typically provide a minimum guaranteed return over the life of the contract. At the time that the owner chooses to terminate the contract, the cash surrender value is compared to a second value calculated using the minimum guaranteed return and the higher of the two values is paid to the annuity owner.

OPTION – A contract which conveys to its holder the right, but not the obligation, to buy or sell something at a specified price on or before a given date. After this given date the option ceases to exist. Insurers typically buy options to provide for the excess interest potential. Options may be American style whereby they may be exercised at any time prior to the given date, or they may have to be exercised only during a specified window. Options that may only be exercised during a specified period are European-style options.

OPTION RISK – Most insurers create the potential for excess interest in an indexed annuity by buying options. Say that you could buy a share of stock for $50. If you bought the stock and it rose to $60 you could sell it and net a $10 profit. But, if the stock price fell to $40 you'd have a $10 loss. Instead of buying the actual stock, we could buy an option that gave us the right to buy the stock for $50 at any time over the next year. The cost of the option is $2. If the stock price rose to $60 we would exercise our option, buy the stock at $50 and make $10 (less the $2 cost of the option). If the price of the stock fell to $40, $30 or $10, we wouldn't use the option and it would expire. The loss is limited to $2 – the cost of the option.

PARTICIPATION RATE – The percentage of positive index movement credited to the annuity. If the index methodology determined that the index increased 10 percent and the indexed annuity participated in 60 percent of the increase, it would be said that the contract has a 60 percent participation rate. Participation rates may also be expressed as asset fees or yield spreads.

POINT-TO-POINT – A crediting method measuring index move-ment from an absolute initial point to the absolute end point for a period. An index had a period starting value of 100 and a period ending value of 120. A point-to-point method would record a positive index movement of 20 [120-100] or a 20 percent positive movement [(120-100)/100]. Point-to-point usually refers to an-nual periods; however the phrase is also used instead of term end point to refer to multiple year periods.

PREMIUM BONUS – A premium bonus is additional money that is credited to the accumulation account of an annuity policy under certain conditions.

PUT OPTION *(ALSO SEE <u>CALL OPTION</u>)* – Gives the holder the right to sell an underlying security or index at a specified price on or before a given date.

QUALIFIED ANNUITIES *(QUALIFIED MONEY)* – Qualified annuities are annuities purchased for funding an IRA, 403(b) tax-deferred annuity or other type of retirement arrangements. An IRA or qualified retirement plan provides the tax deferral. An annuity contract should be used to fund an IRA or qualified retirement plan to benefit from an annuity's features other than tax deferral, including the safety features, lifetime income payout option and death benefit protection.

REQUIRED MINIMUM DISTRIBUTION *(RMD)* – The amount of money that Traditional, SEP and SIMPLE IRA owners and qualified plan participants must begin distributing from their retirement accounts by April 1 following the year they reach age 70.5. RMD amounts must then be distributed each subsequent year.

RETURN FLOOR – Another way of saying minimum guaranteed return.

ROTH IRA – Like other IRA accounts, the Roth IRA is simply a holding account that manages your stocks, bonds, annuities, mutual funds and CD's. However, future withdrawals (including earnings and interest) are typically tax-advantaged once the account has been open for five years and the account holder is age 59.5.

RULE OF 72 – Tells you approximately how many years it takes a sum to double at a given rate. It's handy to be able to figure out, without using a calculator, that when you're earning a 6 percent return, for example, by dividing 6 percent into 72, you'll find that it takes 12 years for money to double. Conversely, if you know it took a sum twelve years to double you could divide 12 into 72 to determine the annual return (6 percent).

SIMPLE INTEREST *(ALSO SEE COMPOUND INTEREST)* – Interest is only earned on the principal balance.

SPLIT ANNUITY – A split annuity is the term given to an effective strategy that utilizes two or more different annuity products – one designed to generate monthly income and the other to restore the original starting principal over a set period of time.

STANDARD & POOR'S 500 *(S&P 500)* – The most widely used external index by fixed indexed annuities. Its objective is to be a benchmark to measure and report overall U.S. stock market performance. It includes a representative sample of 500 common stocks from companies trading on the New York Stock Exchange, American Stock Exchange, and NASDAQ National Market System. The index represents the price or market value of the underlying stocks and does not include the value of reinvested dividends of the underlying stocks.

STOCK MARKET INDEX – A report created from a type of statistical measurement that shows up or down changes in a specific financial market, usually expressed as points and as a percentage, in a number of related markets, or in an economy as a whole (i.e. S&P 500 or New York Stock Exchange).

SURRENDER CHARGE – A charge imposed for withdrawing funds or terminating an annuity contract prematurely. There is no industry standard for surrender charges, that is, each annuity product has its own unique surrender charge schedule. The charge is usually expressed as a percentage of the amount withdrawn prematurely from the contract. The percentage tends to decline over time, ultimately becoming zero.

TRADITIONAL IRA – See IRA (Individual Retirement Account)

TERM END POINT – Crediting methods measuring index movements over a greater timeframe than a year or two. The opposite of an annual reset method. Also referred to as a term point-to-point method. Say that the index value was at 100 on the first day of the period. If the calculated index value was at 150 at the end of the period the positive index movement would be 50 percent (150-100/100). The company would credit a percentage of this movement as excess interest. Index movement is calculated and interest credited at the end of the term and interim movements during the period are ignored.

TERM HIGH POINT *(HIGH WATER MARK)* – A type of term end point structure that uses the highest anniversary index level as the end point. Say that the index value was at 100 on the first day of the period, reached a value of 160 at the end of a contract year during the period, and ended the period at 150. A term high point method would use the 160 value – the highest contract anniversary point reached during the period, as the end point and the gross index gain would be 60 percent (160-100/100). The company would then apply a participation rate to the gain.

TERM YIELD SPREAD – A type of term end point structure which calculates the total index gain for a period, computes the annual compound rate of return deducts a yield spread from the annual rate of return and then recalculates the total index gain for the period based on the net annual rate. Say that an index increased from 100 to 200 by the end of a nine year period. This is the equivalent of an 8 percent compound annual interest rate. If the annuity had a 2 percent term yield spread this would be deducted from the annual interest rate (8 percent-2 percent) and the net rate would be credited to the contract (6 percent) for each of the nine years. Total index gain may also be computed by using the highest anniversary index level as the end point.

VARIABLE ANNUITY – A contract issued by an insurance company offering separate accounts invested in a wide variety of stocks and/or bonds. The investment risk is borne by the annuity owner. Variable annuities are considered securities and require appropriate securities registration.

1035 EXCHANGE – The 1035 exchange refers to the section of tax code that allows annuity owners the flexibility to exchange one annuity for another without incurring any immediate tax liabilities. This action is most often utilized when an annuity holder decides they want to upgrade an annuity to a more favorable one, but they do not want to activate unnecessary tax liabilities that would typically be encountered when surrendering an existing annuity contract.

401(K) ROLLOVER – See IRA Rollover

Made in the USA
Charleston, SC
30 April 2016